AUTHORITY:
A PHILOSOPHICAL
ANALYSIS

EDITED BY
R. Baine Harris

WITH A BIBLIOGRAPHY BY
Richard T. De George

THE UNIVERSITY OF ALABAMA PRESS

University, Alabama

Library of Congress Cataloging in Publication Data
Main entry under title:

Authority: A Philosophical Analysis.

  Bibliography: p.
  Includes index.
  1. Authority.   2. Authority (Religion) I. Harris,
R. Baine, 1927–
BD209.A9   301.15'52'01   75-11666
ISBN 0-8173-6620-2 (cloth)
ISBN 0-8173-6621-0 (paper)

Contents

Contributors

E. MAYNARD ADAMS

E. Maynard Adams, Kenan Professor of Philosophy at the University of North Carolina at Chapel Hill, received the A.B. and M.A. degrees from the University of Richmond, the B.D. degree from Colgate-Rochester Divinity School, and the M.A. and Ph.D. degrees from Harvard University. He has taught at Harvard, Ohio University, and the University of Southern California, and served as chairman of the Department of Philosophy at Chapel Hill from 1960 to 1965. He is the author of a number of articles and books, among which are: *The Fundamentals of General Logic, Ethical Naturalism and the Modern World-View,* and *Philosophy and the Modern Mind.*

MICHAEL D. BAYLES

Michael D. Bayles received a B.A. from the University of Illinois, a M.A. from the University of Missouri, and a Ph.D. from Indiana University. He is currently Professor of Philosophy at the University of Kentucky, having previously taught at the University of Idaho and Brooklyn College of the City University of New York. He is the author of several articles on ethics and political and legal philosophy, and served as editor of collections of essays entitled *Contemporary Utilitarianism, Ethics and Population,* and *Medical Treatment of the Dying: Moral Issues.*

THEODORE M. BENDITT

Theodore M. Benditt received his Ll.B. from the University of Pennsylvania, M.A. from the University of Pennsylvania, and Ph.D. from the University of Pittsburgh. His fields of interest are ethics and legal philosophy, and he has published five articles in the latter. He has taught at Duke University and is currently Assisstant Professor of Philosophy at the University of Southern California.

RICHARD T. DE GEORGE

Richard T. De George, University Professor of Philosophy at the University of Kansas, is currently writing a book on authority. His other works include: *The New Marxism* (Pegasus) and *Soviet Ethics and Morality* (University of Michigan Press).

R. BAINE HARRIS

R. Baine Harris received his B.A. degree from the University of Richmond, B.D. degree from the Southern Baptist Theological Seminary, M.A. from Emory University, and Ph.D. from Temple University. He has taught at the University of Richmond, the Georgia Institute of Technology, Frederick College, Clemson University, Eastern Kentucky University, and Old Dominion University, where he is currently Professor of Philosophy and Chairman of the Department of Philosophy. He is the author of several articles in journals and dictionaries and was editor of a special double issue of *The Southern Journal of Philosophy* on "The Crisis of Authority." He also contributed to and edited a forthcoming volume, *The Significance of Neoplatonism,* and was the founder of the International Society for Neoplatonic Studies, which he now serves as Executive-Director.

IREDELL JENKINS

Iredell Jenkins received the A.B., M.A., and Ph.D. degrees (1937) from the University of Virginia. He studied for a year at the Sorbonne, and has taught at Tulane, Yale, Northwestern, and the University of Alabama, where he is professor and chairman of the Department of Philosophy. His academic honors include a Rockefeller Foundation grant and a fellowship from the American Council of Learned Societies. Contributor to journals, he is a member of the Editorial Board of the *Southern Journal of Philosophy.* His publications include *Art and Human Enterprise* (Harvard University Press, 1958).

REX MARTIN

Rex Martin received his B.A. degree, with honors in History, from Rice University and his M.A. and Ph.D. degrees from Columbia. He also studied in Edinburgh for a year under a grant from the Society for Religion in Higher Education, and in Helsinki for a year as a Fulbright Research Scholar. Currently he is Professor of Philosophy and Chairman of the Department of Philosophy at the University of Kansas. His fields of major interest are political philosophy, philosophy of the social sciences, and philosophy of history, in which he is at present completing a book on explanation and understanding in history.

WADE L. ROBISON

Wade L. Robison received his B.A. with High Honors at the University of Maryland and his Ph.D. at the University of Wisconsin, with a major in Philosophy and a minor in law. He has taught at the University of Wisconsin and at Ohio State University and is at present an Associate Professor of Philosophy at Kalamazoo College. His publications are in the areas of political and social philosophy and the history of modern philosophy. He is currently writing a book on David Hume.

W. H. WERKMEISTER

William Henry Werkmeister received his training in philosophy in Germany and the United States and received his Ph.D. degree from the University of Nebraska. He served as chairman of the Department of Philosophy at the University of Nebraska from 1945 to 1953 and at the University of Southern California from 1954 to 1966. Currently he is Professor Emeritus of Philosophy at Florida State University. In addition to serving as editor of *The Personalist* from 1958 to 1966, his publications include: *The Basis and Structure of Knowledge, An Introduction to Critical Thinking, A History of Philosophical Ideas in America, Theories of Ethics, Man and his Values,* and a two-volume *Historical Spectrum of Value Theories.*

Introduction

R. Baine Harris

ONE of the factors contributing to the current unrest in our society is the breakdown of respect for authority. Authorities are now being challenged in all areas of human life. Institutions are no longer respected just because they are institutions. The church, the school, the family, the state—those traditional bastions of authority— have lost a large amount of the respect that was formerly automatically accorded to them. In almost every country of the world, the young question the views of their elders to a degree never done before.

More is at stake, we believe, than the mere revolt of dissidents. At issue is a change in our way of thinking about the basic nature and function of *authority itself*. We are now witnessing a challenge to the very *idea* of authority. The crisis of authority is more than a reconsideration of how authority should be expressed in society. It extends also to a reconsideration of the *meaning* of authority.

Many of the questions now being asked about the nature and function of authority are quite healthy ones, motivated not from rebellion and revolt, but from a sincere quest to discover the true nature and locus, or *loci*, of authority. What is happening, we think, is the attempt to internalize authority, that is, to shift the basis of its verification from external and public modes to internal and private ones. Such a phenomenon is the natural and normal consequence of the recent attempt to translate democracy into a mass function in society.

1

In our analysis of the current crisis of authority, however, we must separate the analysis of a society in an authority crisis from the analysis of changes in the idea of the nature and function of authority. The essays in this volume deal mainly with the latter. In addition to exploring some of the philosophical implications involved in the present crisis, they investigate the nature and locus of authority, its linguistic meaning, and the meaning and function of its various types: moral, epistemic, political, and religious. It is our hope that they will aid in eliminating some of the confusion that now exists concerning the meaning of the term and that they will also stimulate further investigations of the issues discussed.

The Philosophical Grounds
of the Present Crisis
# of Authority

E. M. Adams

A CRISIS of authority exists.* It is felt in the home, the school, the city, and the nation. Society is believed by many, especially the young, to be unjust and repressive. There is a revolutionary spirit abroad. This is not only true in America but, to some extent, throughout the Western world. No doubt, society is more complex and therefore more demanding as well as more difficult to comprehend, but one may well wonder whether it is by any objective measure less just or more morally repressive than in earlier days. In fact, can we seriously doubt that our American dream has been realized far beyond what our forefathers had any right to expect?

Why, then, the crisis of authority? Some attribute it to increased moral sensitivity and earnestness of the young against the background of cynicism and hypocrisy of the older generation. Moral confusion does pervade the establishment and the strident, shrill voice of the young radical is heard everywhere. But both, I suggest, are symptoms of something much deeper.

The thesis of this paper is that the structure of authority is crumbling in our society not so much because of injustice and repression as

*This article was written in 1969.

3

because of the erosion of its intellectual foundations. The philosophical assumptions on which authority as such, not just the authority of our existing institutions, is founded are being rapidly rejected in our culture, especially by the more self-aware and better-educated of the younger generation, because of the apparent inconsistency of these assumptions with other deep and firm commitments of the modern Western mind.

I shall sketch an analytical normative theory of authority, point up certain philosophical assumptions on which it is based, and explore certain intellectual developments and their resulting patterns of political thought that call these assumptions into question and thereby undermine even the possibility of a structure of authority.

I

We speak of authority in two distinct but related senses. One pertains to beliefs or knowledge which we may call "epistemic" authority; the other to decisions or actions which may be appropriately called "moral authority." With regard to the first, we speak of one as an authority on some subject. What this involves can be put succinctly, for there is no problem about it. To be an authority on a subject is to be in a position to know about it, or in a somewhat stronger sense, to be one whose *business* it is to know about such things, and to have credentials such that others less privileged in relevant ways are justified in accepting his views on the subject, indeed ought to accept his views, even if they are contrary to their own. It is irrational of one to persist in his own ill-founded beliefs about a matter in the face of contrary beliefs of a genuine authority on the subject. The rational thing to do, if one is not an authority on a given subject, is to defer to the beliefs of those who are, for what better grounds can one who is not knowledgeable in a given field have for a belief in that area than that it is the belief of one who is knowledgeable about such matters, especially of one whose business it is to know about such things? This in no way involves shirking one's responsibility for his own thoughts. It is simply a matter of the responsible way of weighing evidence or reasons for beliefs in the process of making up one's mind on a subject.

Authority in the area of decision and action is somewhat more complex. There is, of course, the same kind of authority just mentioned—the authority of experts on skills, marriage counselors, consulting engineers, economic advisers, and the like. The only difference is that such authority concerns know-how or what to do rather than knowledge of facts or what to believe. But just as in the case of belief, in addition to any arguments the authority may give in support of his advice, the fact that he gave the advice counts in its favor and one may be justified in deferring to his superior wisdom. That is, for others the judgment of an authority is at least partially self-warranting. This is not unlike the way in which for a normal person the fact that he has a given perceptual experience counts for its own veridicality. This is not to say that it cannot be overridden by contrary reasons. In like manner, the fact that an authority has a certain view or gives certain advice counts in its favor over and above the reasons that he may have for so thinking or for so advising. The fact that he, knowledgeable and experienced in the field, takes those reasons to justify a given position augments the reasons for the position. The layman who does not know or cannot evaluate the reasons that the authority has for his position has two kinds of reasons for accepting the authority's view or advice: (1) knowing him to be an authority in the field, the layman knows that there probably are good reasons for his view or advice, and (2) he knows that the authority, in assessing the reasons that are available to him, has been led to his position.

But the kind of authority that is peculiar in the area of decision and action concerns the responsibility or the right to decide or to act in such a way that commits others or obligates others to commit themselves accordingly.

A word about decision and action. A decision, the formation of an *intention,* is the acceptance of an imperative much as the formation of a *belief* is the acceptance of a proposition. One can from his own experience and thought, without communication from another, form a belief. But one can form a belief by simply accepting what he he is told is the case. Both may be rationally justified. The fact that so and so told something may be a good reason for believing it, especially if the person who did the telling is an authority in the field. The same is true in the case of decision. One can reach a decision on the basis of his own experience and thought, on the basis of the counsel of another, or by accepting what he is told to do by one who has authority over him. Any of these, it would seem, could be rationally justified.

An action is the fulfillment of, or an effort to fulfill, an accepted imperative. The action is itself properly described only in terms of the intention that structures it.

An authority may have the responsibility or the right not only to decide what another is to do or not to do but actually, in some cases, to act for him as well; e.g., the case of a parent for his child, an officer of an organization for the organization, etc.

To have moral authority, then, is to have an office or position constituted by certain responsibilities and rights, where the rights are areas of freedom required for the fulfillment of the responsibilities, that involves making decisions that obligate certain others, at least *prima facie,* to accept and to comply with them, regardless of what their personal decisions about the matters otherwise would have been. In the very nature of the case, the voice of authority is at least *prima facie* overriding for those subject to or obligated by the authority. Furthermore, the authority, or some other agency whose function it is, has the right and indeed responsibility to enforce compliance. Such is the case with the parent, the teacher, the foreman, the judge, the legislative body, the head of state, etc. What we are concerned with is the rational of moral authority. How can one be obligated by the decision of another in this way? Is authority compatible with freedom?

No one simply as a human being has authority over another. It is always with respect to some special office or position that one holds. The authority of a parent with respect to a minor child, for example, is not simply grounded in a biological fact but in an office defined by certain responsibilities and rights, an office that one may, under some conditions, voluntarily relinquish, and one from which one can be dismissed. Competence to fulfill the responsibilities and to exercise the rights of the office is assumed. The parent has the right and the responsibility to decide for the child and the child is subject to, and is obligated to obey, the parent in those areas in which the child is incompetent to decide for himself. As the child matures and becomes more and more capable of responsible self-direction, the responsibility and authority of the parent diminish accordingly until the office becomes purely honorary.

It is clear, I think, that one important factor in the authority of the parent in relation to his child and in the obligation of the child to accept the decision of his parent and to act on it, even though his own decision, if left unto himself, would have been quite different, is that the parent is in a better position to know what ought to be done and is more likely to make a wiser decision .Even though the child may not comprehend the parent's reasons, he may be justified in believing that as a competent parent he has good reasons for it; furthermore, the fact that the parent, on the basis of whatever reasons he has, made the decision in question counts in favor of the decision; and because it is the business of the parent, by virtue of his office, to make such decisions, it ought to be obeyed by the child unless there are strong counter-reasons. Therefore, from the child's point of view, the rational thing for him to do in most cases, even without taking into account penalties for disobedience, is to accept and to act on the decision of the parent.

Much the same is true for the whole structure of authority. The foreman, the teacher, the policeman, the judge, the legislative body, etc., hold offices constituted by responsibilities and rights that involve making decisions that certian others have *prima facie* overriding obligations to accept and to act on; and in the case of inexcusable disobedience, the authority in question or some other agency has not only the right but a responsibility to impose penalties. If the offices that exercise authority are wisely constituted and if the general competence of office holders is maintained, then those subject to the authority of a particular office have good reasons to comply with the authority in question quite apart from whatever penalties there may be for disobedience.

The penalties serve two functions. The first is educational. They point out in clearly recognizable terms the importance of compliance. The second is to give the person who is not sensitive to other considerations a reason that will move him, for there are compelling reasons for compliance and the authority or some associated agency has the responsibility for obtaining it.

The authority of an office within an organization committed to a limited goal, like that of an educational institution or a business firm, is itself limited. The offices of the organization are constituted by the division of function required for achieving the specific objectives of the organization. Some of these offices will have the responsibility or the right to make decisions for others to execute. It may be assumed that in a well-managed organization responsibility for decision-making is assigned on the basis of relevant knowledge and competence. Maximum penalty for refusal or failure of those subject to such decisions to act on them is expulsion. One makes himself subject to the structure of authority in the organization and he is free to escape from it, even if it may be inconvenient or costly for him to do so.

Political authority is significantly different. The objective of a polity is nothing less than that of the moral enterprise itself, at least so far as life within the society is concerned. Its function is to regulate private and public pursuits for the purpose of securing the rights of individuals and assuring justice for all and to be the agency of society for collective action in pursuit of the common good. Thus *bona fide* government is the voice and arm of morality. Herein lies its peculiar authority. The government of a state, so far as it is the moral voice and agent of the society, has authority over individual and group interest just as one's conscience or moral judgment has authority over one's wants and inclinations. Whenever the government of a society becomes the voice and arm of some faction or special interest group, it ceases to have authority and becomes only a power to be dealt with. We mark this distinction by speaking of *de facto* and *de jure* governments.

The voice of *de jure* government has authority not only over individual or group interests but even over the moral judgment of an individual or group. Here we have to distinguish between one's independent moral judgment about a matter and his judgment in light of the fact that there is a law or decision of government about it. One's independent judgment in a given situation might be that he ought to do A. But taking into account that there is a law against it, he might conclude that he ought not to do A, and this conclusion might be without regard to penalties. Epistemic authority is a factor.

The mere existence of the law under a government with authority indicates that a body of people whose business it is to consider such matters have found reasons that convinced them that such actions were wrong and to such an extent that they should be prohibited by law. This brings additional considerations into the picture that one must weigh in making up one's mind and they may be sufficient to call into question or to reverse one's prior judgment. Even if, after careful deliberation, one's first judgment remains unshaken and he is supported in it by the responsible judgment of many others, the law still has priority over his judgment and should be so recognized by him, for it is the official moral voice of the society. This is not to say that one should never, on the basis of his own judgment, act contrary to the law. But it does mean that the individual who feels that there are compelling reasons in a particular situation for him to go against the law must accept the responsibility of justifying his action before rational men in a court or accept the penalty under the law. Nor does it rule out civil disobedience as a way of protest and reform. If one is informed and rationally convinced that his government has made a grievous error of great magnitude, and if other means of protest and correction have been exhausted or are unavailable, one may be justified to protest by disobedience and acceptance of the penalty involved to call attention to the reasons that already exist for correcting the governmental position. This is just as proper as violating a law in order to get a court case to test the constitutionality of the law itself. But one cannot forcibly resist the government without denying its authority or acknowledging the criminality of one's action. The right of rebellion holds only with regard to a *de facto* government. Only if one's government was systematically and grossly unjust and all established procedures for correction had been exhausted, would one be justified in confronting it with force. But under such circumstances one might even be obligated to do so.

Each one in judging and making decisions has to operate from within his own perspective, defined by his assumptions, beliefs, attitudes, and experiences. Internal to one's perspective, one's decisions and actions may be rationally justified without the perspective itself being defensible. Therefore, we have to distinguish between subjective and objective justification. The first is internal justification only;

the second is this together with justification of one's perspective. The latter is very difficult. Any correcting of one's perspective must be done from within. Perhaps the best we can do is to establish that one perspective is better justified than another. No one has a right to be as sure of the justification of his perspective as of the internal justification of particular judgments and decisions. Given the conflict of perspectives, there is reason for each to accept the perspective of responsible government, especially in a free, enlightened, democratic society. Revolution is a rational option only when a large number of people, on the basis of their own perspectives, become rationally convinced that the perspective of the government is grossly in error and thus systematically perverts its internal decisions and actions. This is a difficult conclusion to defend for the perspective of the government calls into question the correctness of their contrary perspectives just as their perspectives cast doubt upon the perspective of the government. Something of a wide public consensus has to emerge against the perspective of government to make revolution a rational option. But if this should happen in a democratic society, a revolution would not be necessary, for the perspective of the government would itself be changed by the emerging public consensus.

Wisely structured and well functioning political authority does not compromise genuine freedom, for under such conditions the individual or group subject to the authority has good reasons, quite apart from any penalties that might be involved, to comply with its requirements. Freedom would be compromised only if the rational, informed person would have to take into account the penalties in order to find a good reason for compliance. Thus ideally the coercing force of government would be used only against those who grossly fail to do the morally right from their own reasoning. The informed, rational person, acting from his own deliberations, would never feel the external restraint of authority; nor would his beliefs and inner motivations be manipulated and shaped by indoctrination or propaganda. Through knowledge and practical reason one can be free under authority; and without knowledge and practical reason one cannot be free at all. Of course, we never achieve perfection on the part of either political authority or rational citizens. Therefore, perfect freedom under government is never achieved. But we do have more or less freedom. It can be maximized only by increasing the rationality of the government and of the citizenry.

II

The foregoing analytical, normative theory of authority, or something very much like it, has been widely accepted and provides the general moral basis of government and the whole structure of authority in our society. It is formulated in ordinary moral language and involves theoretical moral reasoning. Therefore, it would appear to be something which philosophy of ethics should be responsible to and square itself with rather than the other way around. Neverthless, it is based on certain philosophical assumptions about morality, namely, that there is moral knowledge and that moral disagreements are logical in character and can in principle be resolved by inquiry and rational debate. Any philosophy of ethics that renders these matters intelligible would be consistent with our normative theory of authority; but, for the same reason, any philosophy that rejects these assumptions would thereby undermine not only our normative theory of authority but our institutions and way of life based on it.

Here we find interdependence between philosophy of ethics and and normative thought. This is contrary to a widely accepted view that philosophy of any area of culture, like ethics or science, is responsible to what is done in that area and must render it philosophically intelligible rather than dictate to it or reject it. In dealing with this problem, we need to distinguish between philosophical assumptions and presuppositions. For our purposes, we may regard an assumption as a belief taken for granted and built on as a premise or ground in one's thinking about something else; whereas a presupposition is a necessary condition for the truth or meaningfulness of some sentence. A philosophical assumption on which a scientific or normative theory is built will be presupposed by that theory. But not all philosophical presuppositions make their entry via assumption. Those that do not are the basic ones that provide the ultimate touchstone for philosophy. If a philosophical theory is assumed or taken for granted and thereby shapes the development of a given area of thought, the rejection of that theory in favor of another, whether brought about by philosophical inquiry or otherwise, would work a radical change in the cultural area concerned. On the other hand, the philosophical presuppositions of our primary ways of experiencing, thinking, and talking, those that do not enter the fabric of experience and thought via assumption, cannot be rejected by virtue of inconsistency with philosophical theory. Whenever such inconsistencies arise, so much the worse for the philosophical theory. This is why philosophy must be primarily responsible to the philosophical presuppositions of ordinary discourse rather than those of the specialized disciplines. The latter are more likely to have been influenced by philosophical assumptions; if not by explicit philosophial theory, at least by certain philosophical assumptions pervasive in the culture. Although philosophy does not contradict specific statements in science or judgments in normative thought, it may overturn them by contradicting philosophical assumptions on which they are based.

Our philosophical beliefs or assumptions about the moral enterprise shape our beliefs about the nature and function of government, for government is widely believed to be society's moral agent. The three major patterns of political thought and action in this country, namely, the conservatism of the traditional Republican party, the liberalism of the left wing of the Democratic party, and the radicalism of the New Left, are based on conflicting philosophial assumptions about ethics and therefore are, to a considerable extent, products of the intellectual developments that gave rise to these philosophical assumptions. We shall explore these assumptions, the intellectual developments that gave rise to them, and their compatibility with the assumptions about ethics on which our normative theory of authority is based.

The political conservatism characteristic of the traditional Republican party is a continuation of the political thought of the founding fathers of the eighteenth century, which was shaped largely by their natural law theory of ethics. The natural law theory has had a long and honorable history. It received its classical formulation in the writings of Plato, Aristotle, and the ancient Stoics and played a prominent role in Western thought through the eighteenth century.

The position holds that everything is of a natural kind; that everything has an objective nature or essence. In other words, the essential or defining properties of a thing are not relative to some arbitrary or pragmatically determined classificatory system. They are not language dependent, but rather the language of natural kinds is responsible to objective, independent natural kinds and their essences. Our concepts of natural kinds may be correct or in error. When correct, they constitute our most fundamental kind of knowledge.

The objective nature or essence of a thing is normative in structure. It embodies a normative or prescriptive law that defines for it its proper function, state or condition. The form of the concept of a thing, according to this theory, is not, as we are accustomed to think today, "anything is a ϕ if and only if it is F, G. and H"; but rather, "anything is a ϕ if and only if it is F, and G, and ought to be H. Here is the natural law of the thing, the normative law that is in its nature. Thus, to say that such and such is natural for a certain kind of thing is to say that it is *normal*, that it is the way that kind of thing ought to be by virtue of its very nature. Accordingly, what is natural is good, and what is unnatural is bad. It is difficult for us, steeped in the provincialism of the nineteenth and twentieth centuries, to understand this way of thinking, for our scientific naturalism has long since rejected the view that there are objective values and even that there are objective essences.

A further thesis of natural law ethics is that reason is not merely a critical faculty to assess our experiences and to order the data thereby obtained, but that it is in its own right data-gathering and knowledge-yielding. It is, according to the theory, through reason alone, the mind's eye, that we can grasp and know abstract entities and their necessary relationships, including the objective nature or essence of things. Therefore, there are self-evident normative truths. They are regarded as parallel with the truths of logic and mathematics.

There is, according to the theory, a normative law or imperative inherent in human nature that defines for man a way of life. To be a man, it is said, is, as it were, to have an office, a position, defined by the imperative to live so that one would stand justified under rational criticism. By virtue of this responsibility, man has certain natural rights, certain areas of freedom he is entitled to and must have if he is to have the opportunity to fulfill the primary responsibility of his office as a human being.

The principles of reason, according to the theory, define the rational life. Logic is concerned with the principles of reason pertaining to thought and inquiry; ethics with the principles of reason in relation to human action. In both cases, the principles are thought of as self-evident normative truths discovered by reason itself. They are to life what the rules of a game are to the game. They are regulatory only. They specify the permitted, the prohibited, and the required moves. Within these limits one may work out his own strategy for achieving his objective. Most of one's reasons for believing and for acting are nonlogical and nonethical. Experience and interest provide them.

On this view, freedom is not a matter of being able to do what one wants to do, nor to have what one wants or even needs; but rather a matter of being able to exercise without interference the rights and privileges of the office of a human being in one's efforts to fulfill the responsibilities of the office. When anyone is restrained or coerced by an unethical act of another, his freedom has been violated. A free society is one in which life is within and regulated by the *a priori* ethical principles. It is a matter of the game of life being played according to the rules.

On the assumption that government is the agency of ethics in society, the proper function of government, according to the natural law theory of ethics, is to define clearly how the *a priori* principles of ethics apply to the conditions of its society and to referee the activities of individuals and institutions to guarantee freedom for all to live under their own direction within the limits of the basic ethical norms. It would be a gross violation of its own nature for a government to enter the game itself in trying to promote the specific objectives of individuals, groups, or other institutions. This, I submit, is still the foundation of much conservative political thought in the United States.

As general rationalistic epistemological assumptions gave way to empiricism under the impact of empirical science, the natural law theory of ethics was rejected for the most part, and therefore the normative political thought based on it was undermined. Without the assumption that reason is itself an epistemic power in its own right, modern empiricism maintained that all the data on which the house of knowledge is built are obtained by sensory experience or intro-spection and consists of facts, existences, or occurrences. Concepts were regarded as not discovered but pragmatically formed or made for ordering and structuring the empirical data, and therefore con-venient or useful rather than true or correct. It follows that essences and necessities cannot be objective, but must be language dependent. It also follows that descriptive-explanatory knowledge is value free both with respect to the internal structure of its concepts and its statements. Thus values, along with essences and necessities, are ex-cluded from the objective world and value language given a subjecti-vistic interpretation. Our institutions and way of life, once believed to be grounded in and justified by the cosmic order or the value struc-ture of reality, are cut loose from all ontological foundations. Many saw in this a new freedom—the end of *a priori* ethics, moral abso-lutes, fixed institutions, the right way of life, and the like, and the opportunity for experimentation.

The dominant empiricistic theory of ethics that emerged in the eighteenth and nineteenth centuries was utilitarianism. It drew a sharp distinction between what we may call theoretical and practical knowledge. The first concerns what is the case and why it is so; the second relates to desire, volition, and action. All value knowledge, including ethics, was allocated to the latter.

Classical utilitarianism, and by this I mean primarily Bentham and Mill, maintained that for something to be good in itself is for it to be desired for its own sake and for something to be bad in itself is for it to be avoided for its own sake. Furthermore, no one, Bentham and Mill claimed, desires anything for its own sake but his own pleasure; and no one avoids anything for its own sake but his own pain. From this they concluded that only pleasure and the absence of pain are good in themselves, and only pain is bad in itself. If they had been more careful, they would have said that what each calls "good in itself" is what he himself avoids for its own sake. Thus what each acknowledges to be good in itself is his own pleasure and the absence of his own pain; and what each acknowledges to be bad in itself is his own pain. Whatever else one counts as good is regarded as a means to one's pleasure or the elimination of one's pain; and whatever else one counts as bad is regarded as a cause of one's pain or the elimination of one's pleasure.

It should be remarked that the principle that each man desires for its own sake only his own pleasure etc. is not a contingent psychological law. Bentham and Mill do not operate as though an exception were a possibility. What is at issue here is a theory of practical reasons which is parallel with a theory of empirical data. The contention that one's pleasure and pain are the only primary reasons one can have in the deliberation of actions has the same kind of foundation as the Humean thesis that the only empirical evidence one can have consists of one's own sense-impressions.

For the utilitarian, the concepts of 'ought' and 'right' apply only to actions as means of maximizing the pleasure and minimizing the pain of the agent concerned. Ordinary deliberation by an individual is in terms of maximizing his own happiness, or net sum of pleasure. But moral reasoning is from the perspective of the society of which one is a member, and the most inclusive moral perspective embraces all mankind. From the moral point of view, the pleasure of each is good in itself and the pain of each is bad in itself, and what is morally right or ought to be done is that action which conforms to a pattern of behavior that maximized the net happiness of all concerned in such a way that each can expect to benefit from it as a general practice in the society. In other words, moral deliberation is that of society as an agent.

Government is the only agent whose natural perspective is the moral point of view. Government of a limited society may, of course, make for a closed morality. This is why, on utilitarian grounds, the jurisdiction of a government should embrace the functioning society and not arbitrarily limit the community. Whenever the government of a society operates from any perspective other than the moral, it thereby loses its "authority."

Under the natural law theory, as we recently observed, freedom was conceived in terms of the human objective. To be a man, it was held, is to have an office constituted by the imperative to be rational, to stand justified under rational criticism in experience, thought, and action. Human rights, accordingly, are those areas in which one must be left free to operate in one's own way if he is to have an opportunity to fulfill his responsibilities as a human being. On the utilitarian view, freedom is also conceived in relation to the human objective. But the objective of one's life is taken to be the greatest net sum of pleasure and the objective of society (the moral objective) is conceived as the maximum net sum of pleasure for all. The rights of individuals pertain to what everyone must have in order to maximize the net sum of pleasure for all. This includes not only areas of freedom in which one acts at one's own discretion but also possession and use of things that give pleasure and eliminate pain. To be free, to enjoy one's full rights, on this view, one must have access to certain minimum means of the good life, the minimum varying with the conditions of the society.

The utilitarian agrees with the natural law theorist that the end of government is identical with that of the moral enterprise, but, as we have seen, they disagree about what that end is. For the utilitarian, it is a matter of maximizing the net sum of pleasure for all concerned through patterns of behavior that all can expect to benefit from. The emphasis here is on empirically discovered ways of maximizing pleasure and minimizing pain. The government, on this conception, is not merely a referee of private pursuits, but may be required to reconstitute the institutions of society and the way of life of people in experimentation to find the most effective ways of promoting the happiness of the people. There is little doubt that the utilitarian conception of ethics gave rise to, or at least made possible, socialistic and welfare theories of the state in the nineteenth and twentieth centuries and that it has been the foundation of our own political liberalism in the United States.

Utilitarianism has always had a problem about the authority of the moral perspective and thus of government over the individual. There is no clear resolution of how the egoistic individual can gain the moral perspective. Although there is moral knowledge, there are no moral values or reasons as such for the individual to take into account in his deliberations; that is, there are no moral considerations that in and of themselves count for or against a proposed action in the sense of moving or restraining the agent. Bentham says that everyone, by the natural constitution of the human frame, judges actions of himself and others, even if he does not deliberate his own, by the principle of utility. Thus the principle is given only a *de facto* or existential status, not one of validity. This does not solve the problem of the authority of the moral judgment over one's prudential judgment. The moral "reasons" have to be cashed in terms of or reduced to egoistic reasons in order to have weight with the individual. No doubt the happiness of others gives most people pleasure and the suffering of others gives them pain and therefore have utility value for them. Also the approval of others gives pleasure and their disapproval pain. But if any individual does not derive pleasure and pain from such sources, he is not in any sense in error or in need of correction. He is simply different from most. Furthermore, these, according to Bentham, do not provide sufficient reasons for any one to live within the limits of the morally right. The government must provide a system of rewards and penalties so that each, on the basis of his egoistic reasons, conforms to the morally right. Mill put more emphasis on social conditioning, based on man's natural social feelings, so that individuals would find more pleasure in the socially beneficial and more pain in the socially detrimental. In any case, it seems that for the utilitarian the individual has to be either manipulated or coerced by society in order for him to live within the limits of either morality or government. While morality is on the side of government, it cannot impart authority to government, for it is itself lacking in authority over egoistic interests. Therefore, there is no way, on the utilitarian account, to achieve full "freedom" of the individual under government by increasing the rationality or responsibleness of the government and of the citizenry as in the case of the natural law theory. But we must note that "freedom" means something different for the utilitarian, namely, full enjoyment of certain minimum means of happiness. This may not be incompatible with a certain amount of manipulation and coercion. Perhaps freedom in this sense can best be achieved under government.

The problem of the authority of moral judgments under the utilitarian analysis is a strong indication that the theory is in error. It was just this problem that was back of Moore's naturalistic fallacy argument against all reductionistic theories of value language. According to Moore, one can acknowledge that X is the "morally right" thing for him to do, as this would be interpreted by the utilitarian, while still asking "Ought I to do X?" There would be no inconsistency in saying: "X is in conformity with a pattern of behavior that, of all alternatives, tends to maximize pleasure and minimize pain, etc., but I ought not to do X; it would be wrong for me to do X." The problem of authority is also related to what Charles Stevenson was getting at in his contention that value judgments are necessarily tied in with feelings, emotions, and attitudes. According to the utilitarian theory, one can say, "I know that it would be morally wrong for me to do X, but I have no reason for not doing it and I am fully for going ahead with it." Stevenson pointed out that there is an absurdity in saying, "X is wrong but I am fully in favor of doing it" just as there is in saying, "President Roosevelt died in 1945 but I don't believe it." A value judgment, he contended, expresses one's value attitude and the acceptance of a value judgment forms a value attitude. One cannot divorce his value judgments from his emotions, which are his springs of action. Purely factual statements are not essentially involved with feelings in this way. Therefore, it is argued, any reduction of value judgments to factual statements is an error.

Moore took such arguments to establish that there are values in an objective, irreducible sense in the form of non-natural or non-empirical properties and that the human mind is capable of knowing them, but he never offered an epistemological account of our knowledge of such values that the modern empiricistic mind could accept. The utilitarians had tried to make a case for moral knowledge without admitting that there are moral values in any unique sense. Moore and Stevenson had shown that moral knowledge requires moral values in an irreducible sense. But professional philosophers and the culture at large, for the most part, have gone contrary to Moore. Rather than admit that there are values distinct from facts, they have denied that there is moral or any form of value knowledge.

The emotivist and the existentialist theories of value language are the most prevalent today. In its simplest form, the emotive theory holds that a value judgment expresses or shows the feeling, sentiment, or attitude of the speaker toward what the judgment is about and that it tends to elicit a similar response from his audience. Emotive states are taken to be original existences, casually produced by one's knowledge of or beliefs about facts. Any reasoning that can be done about value differences pertain to the factual beliefs involved. One's feelings, sentiments, and attitudes as such only exist; they cannot be correct or in error and thus cannot be reasoned about. The existentialist differs from the emotivist primarily in that he subscribes to a voluntaristic rather than a casual theory of the emotions. He takes a value judgment to express one's volition or decision about something. Moral judgments are said to express the speaker's life-constituting decisions and thus define his whole way of life. Such judgments cannot be backed by reasons, for practical reasoning can only take place within a life style. Therefore, they are neither correct nor in error, valid nor invalid. Only two kinds of questions can be raised about such a decision and the judgment that expresses it. First, was it his decision? Or was it the decision of someone else or of society? Second, was it an informed decision? Was it made with his eyes open to the facts? Only one's own informed decision is authentic. All others are condemned. The emphasis is on complete autonomy of the individual.

Good-reasons moral philosophy may be regarded by some as a third position, but all versions of it with which I am acquainted reduce to either emotivism or existentialism. The essence of the theory is that a moral judgment can be backed by reasons and that such arguments can be evaluated. The reasons are factual premises. One group maintains that ultimately for a factual statement to be a reason for an ethical judgment is for the comprehension of the fact stated by it to move or to incline one to accept the ethical judgement and, in appropriate situations, to do what it enjoins. If one is not so moved or inclined by comprehension of the fact in question, there is no sense in which he can be said to be in error or to have failed to see something that is there. He is simply different and there the matter must rest. This, I say, is not basically different from the emotivist position.

Another group maintains that no factual statement is a reason for an ethical conclusion except in conjunction with an imperative premise so that the two, perhaps with others, logically entail the ethical conclusion. The ultimate imperative premise that makes such reasoning possible comes into the picture by a decision of principle that defines a way of life. It itself cannot be backed by reasons of any kind. One's basic imperatives that define his way of life, insofar as he is a free authentic person, are adopted by a free decision without reasons or guidelines. This kind of good-reasons moral philosopher is at one with the existentialist.

The emotive good-reasons position is basically a liberalization of the classical utilitarian theory of reasons. For the utilitarian, it will be recalled, only one's own pleasure or what produces it moves one positively and only one's pain or what produces it moves one negatively. For the emotive good-reasons ethicist, the comprehension of any fact may move one either way. However, it is assumed that as a matter of fact people respond in fairly uniform ways. But the position is open to the possibility that some people react emotively in radically different ways at different times and from other people.

On this position, there is no problem of freedom for one under government so long as he is moved independently of the government's policies and laws by his own comprehension of the facts to act in conformity with the prescriptions of government or so long as he can by argument, without appeal to penalties, be brought to concur with the government. But if he responds differently to the facts of the case, which is always an open possibility, according to the theory, there is no way in which it can be said that either is in error. Therefore, the person who disagrees with the government has no rational basis for seeking reform; nor does the government have any rational basis for claiming that the recalcitrant citizen is in error and in need of correction. Therefore, the government cannot claim validity for its own position; only that it is its own. There is no rational or logical disagreement between the government and the individual. The government might try to point up "reasons" why, in such a conflict, the individual should yield to the government. Some might be moved by such considerations, but some might not. It is all a matter of how they are causally affected by comprehension of the facts cited. Those unmoved by such arguments remain in conflict with the government, but they cannot be said in any way to be in error. Therefore, according to the normative theory of authority with which we began, for the government to use force to obtain compliance would be a matter of pure force without authority. It would be arbitrary compromise of their freedom, for they were not in any significant sense obligated by the prescriptions of the government and the enforcement could not be justified before the bar of reason in such a way that any ideal informed, rational man (one who would not make a mistake) would concur in it as right.

In fact, on the causal theory of emotions, it is difficult to see how moral reasoning itself is anything other than causal manipulation. And if so, wherein lies the authority of government, conceived in the manner of our normative theory, even where the government could in principle obtain compliance by moral argument? It seems that moral authority necessarily involves epistemic authority in the field of values, which is not possible, according to the emotive good-reasons theory. But this is, I believe, the most satisfactory theory of ethics that has been proposed from within modern naturalism.

The existentialist theory is the one that is carrying the day, at least in the popular culture. It is, I suggest, at the heart of our present crisis of authority and the New Left political movements. If a person's authentic moral judgments express his unguided and unbacked life-constituting decisions that cannot in any way be faulted, except as not one's own or as not fully informed, then, in the very nature of the case, there can be no authority. No one can be obligated by a decision of another. No one has the right or the responsibility to make decisions for others to execute. Freedom is a matter of having no obligations, of following no conventions, of being under no laws. The ideal of spiritual perfection is that of being subject to one's own will alone.

On this view, one's moral judgments are very personal and precious. They are not subject to discussion nor debate. One does not try to convince others of them. One simply acts on them. All "authority" collapses into a pure power structure. All institutionalized livng, all conventional morality, all law enforcement become repressive. The individual feels himself smothered and destroyed by society. If people are to be free and fully human, society and government must be destroyed. Chaos must be created. Out of it free people may emerge. The only way they can live and work together is in a participatory democracy in which each participates by his own decision, free to withdraw from any activity at his own will, and unobligated by the decision or act of anyone else or any group.

This, I submit, is the philosophy of the radical New Left in American politics. It is not some aberration of the younger generation, but a logical development of the naturalistic intellectual commitments deep within the modern mind. These ideas have been working themselves out among intellectuals for a long time as our culture has struggled toward consistency. They are just now achieving a wide popularity among the younger generation by virtue of the success of our educational institutions.

III

What I have tried to do in this paper is to formulate the normative theory of authority in terms of which the structure of authority in society is validated; point up some of the philosophical assumptions about ethics on which this normative theory is based; review the philosophical assumptions about ethics that underlie the three major patterns of political thought and action in our society today and explore their implications for the normative theory of authority and the structure of authority grounded in it; and locate the major intellectual commitments in our culture that have given rise to these different philosophical views about ethics.

My findings are these. Our structure of authority is based on a normative theory grounded in the philosophical assumption that ethics involves knowledge of objective values in such a way that ethical differences are, at least in principle, subject to resolution by rational inquiry and debate. Conservative political thought characteristic of the traditional Republican has, to a considerable extent, remained committed to the rationalistic theory of ethical knowledge assumed by the founding fathers and consequently has encountered no real problem about authority. But the culture at large, under the impact of empirical science and modern education, has, for the most part, rejected epistemological rationalism in favor of scientific empiricism or naturalism. Political liberalism such as that of the left wing of the Democratic party has, by and large, operated on the utilitarian conception of ethics, which was for a long time widely accepted as a satisfactory philosophical theory of ethics from within the perspective of empiricism. While admitting that there is moral knowledge, the utilitarian denies that there are objective values in any unique sense or distinctive moral reasons that move individuals. Therefore, the utilitarian theory of ethics is, in a subtle way, inconsistent with the philosophical assumption which underlies our normative theory of authority. In fact, even moral judgments as such do not, according to the utilitarian, obligate the individual in the sense of providing him with constraining reasons for action. The difficulties utilitarianism and similar reductionistic theories of ethics have with the problem of authority led to non-cognitivistic theories of ethics, all of which are inconsistent with our normative theory of authority. This has resulted in rejection not only of the normative theory, but of the structure of authority it validated. Thus, our present New Left radical politics and our general crisis of authority are fruits of the movement of the modern mind toward consistency from within its naturalistic perspective.

In closing, let me say that if my diagnosis of our present crisis of authority is correct, there is no easy solution. Getting out of foreign wars, abolishing the draft, solving the poverty and race problems, and the like may lessen the strains but will not get at the basic difficulties. If we insist on the correctness of the naturalistic perspective of the modern mind, we may have to live under what we can only regard as a repressive power structure or revert to primitive conditions that would make possible participatory democracy. My own conclusion about the matter is that the modern naturalistic mind is seriously deranged by false philosophical assumptions about human epistemic powers and that the only solution is through cultural therapy by philosophical analysis that exposes and corrects these errors. Although I see no hope for reviving the rationalistic theory of ethics, I have elsewhere argued for a realistic theory of empirical value knowledge. If such a theory is correct, our normative theory of authority is still viable, but our scientific naturalism is oveturned.

Wide acceptance of these conclusions would bring about a profound cultural revolution. Never was the challenge to philosophers so great as today and never was the philosopher's work more important. Nothing less than civilization itself is at stake.

Authority:
Its Nature
and Locus

Iredell Jenkins

I

A CONSPICUOUS and significant feature of the contemporary scene is the intense urge for social reform and melioration. This is perhaps most obvious in the case of the so-called "emergent nations" or "newly independent states." But it is at least as pressing with regard to race relations in the United States. It is at the heart of the worldwide phenomena of "student unrest" and the New Left. The underprivileged everywhere voice the same plea, though in a largely inarticulate manner. And all of those who in their various ways are disenchanted with the quality of life in an industrial society and a materialistic culture likewise clamor for radical change. In the face of this much discontent and discord, it is the part of expedience as well as wisdom to undertake a close analysis of the problems involved in large scale social reform.

I think that the most critical of these problems centers around the concept of 'authority.' The indispensable condition for effective social reform is the ability to institute an authority that is adequate to the circumstances it faces and acceptable to the people whose lives are to be changed. It is not enough to draw up even the most detailed and comprehensive proposals, projects, plans, and programs. By themselves, these are merely promises. What is required to give them substance is an authority that can mediate the present and the future, can tailor ideal forms to actual conditions, and can arouse the enthusiasm and allegiance of the people it seeks to lead. It is the lack of such authority that is at the bottom of most of our troubles. This is everywhere apparent; it manifests itself in the "generation gap," the "credibility gap," the distrust of blacks for whites, the suspicion of natives toward foreigners, the ineffectiveness of such international organizations as the United Nations and the European Common Market, the attitudes of labor and management toward one another, and the current bad name of that notorious phantom, The Establishment. In all of these cases, our efforts at reform fail spectacularly, even when they are motivated by good will and directed by sound intelligence. And the root cause of these failures is our inability to identify and establish an authority that has a close acquaintance with its milieu and enjoys the confidence of its people.

If this diagnosis is correct, then an analysis of the nature and locus of authority is relevant and pressing. In carrying out this analysis, I have taken as my paradigm case the familiar effort to reorganize and moderize those tribal societies that have just become nations and are seeking to become industrial civilizations on the Western pattern. And it is my claim that the authority that is to plan and guide this reform—this quest for a higher level of value achievement—must have its primary locus within the society that is being reformed: for it is only an authority that is so based that can be kept both sensitive and responsible to the needs and aspirations—the real values—of the society. But I would maintain that these same considerations apply to all reform movements. Whether the contemplated reform concerns race relations, education and the role of students, international organization, economic adjustment, or the moral reorientation of society:—in all of these cases alike, the necessary condition for success is that those whose way of life is to be changed must themselves generate, establish, and accept the leadership that is to effect this change.

This means that we need to give the phrase "social reform" its full weight and meaning. We are so accustomed to the idea that we take it quite casually and think of it on the model of our extensive accomplishments in refashioning the material world. Once we have a large control in reshaping physical substances, and even plants and animals, we feel that we can do the same with societies, and by the same methods: by mastering their structures and functions and then operating on these from the outside. That is, we treat social groups as though they were completely passive and plastic, so that we can remake them at will to patterns of our own choosing. And this is simply not the case. Any society or social group has a mode of existence that is peculiarly its own, with habits, beliefs, practices, values, and purposes that make up its substance. We cannot remake these arbitrarily and by dictation. We can only reform them gradually and by persuasion. That is, the members of the group must be led to understand and want the new form—the reform—that is being proposed to them. So social change must be internally wrought, not externally imposed.

The argument in support of this thesis hinges upon the two key concepts of *authority* and *value*. And it is the latter of these concepts that has the primary claim on our attention, because it is considerations of value that play a dominant role in determining both the course and the success of social reforms. It is precisely on this point, I think, that current opinion is often mistaken in theory and so is led to failure in practice. The natural inclination of both the "practical politician" and the "professional diplomat" is to identify some locus of power—actual or potential—and then to confer upon this authority to institute the proposed reforms. That is, a program of "social reorganization" is first planned *in absentia*, and then local agents are appointed to carry it out. Insofar as politicians and diplomats are accustomed to operating within an established social order, based on purposes that are held in common and a government that is acknowledged as sovereign, this approach to the problem of social change is understandable. For under these conditions it does indeed appear that "authority" is an independent variable—an autonomous force—that is used to define and create "values." But the repeated failures of this technique when employed as a tool for the "modernization" of various "newly emergent nations" should have persuaded us that it is mistaken.

The character of this mistake is simple, but basic; it rests upon a transposition of the true roles of "authority" and "value." It has been widely assumed that the goals of social change are already clearly known and universally accepted; and that the key to reform lies solely in the establishment of an authority that can overcome the narrow but entrenched forces that oppose such reforms. We have taken for granted the values to be sought, identifying these with the ideal content of our tradition: a carefully drawn Constitution and Bill of Rights, democratic processes, parliamentary government, public education, individual ownership of property, personal freedom, economic growth, industrializaton, and so on. We have supposed that everyone must, in the natural course of things, aspire to these same goods, and that these popular aspirations are frustrated only by the opposition of vested interests. Acting on these assumptions, we have concentrated our efforts on trying to find or found an authority that can dethrone the despots and realize the will of the people. In sum, we have relied too largely upon the lever of authority as the instigator of social change; and we have forgotten that a clear and compelling sense of values—of common purposes and goals—is the fulcrum without which the force of this lever, however great, is altogether impotent. Lacking this basis in shared values, the appeal to authority can create only winds of discord. In fact, as I hope to show later, this is not even "an appeal to authority" but merely "the application of power." Given a fulcrum, even the most makeshift lever can accomplish something; while the longest lever imaginable is useless without a fulcrum.

II

It is now time to replace metaphor with argument. We can begin with the truism that the effort to effect social change is premised on the assumption that this change will constitute an improvement: that is, that it will enhance the realization of values for the members of the society—or social group—that is being reformed. This is the reason for undertaking the transition, which is certain to be painful and laborious for all concerned. This being the case, the question, who has the authority to direct this change, refers us to a more basic question: Who is in the best position to discern and promote the values to which the society aspires? What individuals, groups, or institutions can most effectively accomplish the transition from one mode of life—one set of values—to another that will be more rewarding?

All of this is to say that the proper disposition of authority is not primarily a legal or political issue, but rather a moral and social one. It is only after a determination of the ideal ends to be sought and the actual conditions that one confronts, that problems of legal and political organizations can receive intelligent consideration. Hence any program of social reform must be based upon a careful assessment of the values that are at stake, in both the old order and the new, and of the means that are available to secure them. And this clearly requires, as its support, a theoretical understanding of the nature of value, the conditions of value-occurrence, and the process of value-realization. So these fundamental issues must be our first concern. More specifically, we require answers to these three questions:

I. What is *"value"*? What is the nature and the *mode of being* of "values"? More concretely, exactly what do we mean when we say that land reform, rural credit, universal education, and modernization in general are "values"? What characteristics do we hereby attribute to these things and situations?

II. What are the conditions of value achievement? What is the structure of the process through which values are realized? What requirements must be met, and what steps must be taken, if our efforts to secure values are to be successful?

III. What is involved in the transition from one mode of social order, based on and providing certain values, to a different social order, supposedly yielding greater value? How can we assure that our proposed reforms will be effective and will constitute improvements—that modernization will be a real enrichment of life, and not merely a supercial face-lifting or even a fiasco?

At the very start of this inquiry, in dealing with the question of the nature of value, it is first necessary to draw a distinction and then to avoid two opposing errors that this distinction often invites. The distinction itself is very familiar and deceptively simple: it differentiates between intrinsic or final value on the one hand and extrinsic or instrumental value on the other. The intrinsically valuable is that which stands on its own feet and needs no further justification: it is the end sought by action, the consummation achieved; it is good or worthwhile or desirable in itself, needing no completion; in a word, it is its own excuse for being. The extrinsically valuable is that which supports and sustains the occurence of intrinsic value: it is the means to an end, the things and devices we employ to achieve our purposes; it is good and desirable to the extent that it serves as an instrument to procure final values.

It is the generally held opinion in modern philosophy that intrinsic values are exclusively occurrences in experience, and have their primary locus in human consciousness. Final values—values in the strict sense—reside in activities and the enjoyments that inhere in and accompany these: they are functions of the exercise of man's abilities and talents; and they reflect the realization of various of man's potentialities. Such values exist only as consummations, never as finished products or secured conditions: as Aristotle put it long ago, happiness is an activity, not a state; as modern terminology puts it, values are pleasures, enjoyments, delights, satisfactions, or gratified interests. In brief and in essence, value is always an accomplishment, never a *fait accompli.*

Extrinsic values are all of those "things"—in the broadest possible sense of the term—that we use to support our activities and to secure our enjoyments. The catalogue of such instrumental values is long and varied: it comprises the whole range of physical objects with which we carry on transactions—tools, conveniences, works of art, animals, even other human beings; the moral and practical rules that we follow and inculcate; the norms we hold to and the ideals we pursue; the skills and techniques that we develop; the situations and states-of-affairs that we seek to procure; the institutions and organizations that we establish; the practices that we refine and transmit. All such items—including of course "land reform," and "rural credit," "universal education," and "modernization" in general—are instrumental values: they are only provisionally and potentially valuable, and their actual value depends upon their success in promoting the human achievement of intrinsic values.

I think that this distinction is sound, and I subscribe in general to the terms in which it is drawn; though I would temper this agreement with certain refinements and reservations that need not concern us here. But what must concern us are the errors that are often induced by the seeming simplicity of this distinction. These are as simple as the distinction itself, and consist in becoming so intent upon one of these modes of value that the other is lost from sight. We may, in the one case, become so obsessed with final values—with the desires, pleasures, and satisfactions that people claim—that we forget the dependence of these upon the whole complex of instrumental values. We are then apt to conclude that whatever values people enjoy—or that we think they ought to and naturally must enjoy—both can and should be made immediately accessible to them, without consideration of the availability of the necessary extrinsic values. When stated thus in naked abstractness, this conclusion is transparently fallacious and would hardly fool a greedy child. Yet we are often lured into its trap, under the pressure of concrete claims supported by strong emotions. We may, on the other hand, become so engrossed in the manipulation of instrumental values—in providing the material, technical, and institutional conditions that are conspicuously lacking—that we forget that these are only means to human satisfactions, and are altogether sterile unless they can be successfully exploited. We may then conclude that if we can only secure these conditions, then the quality of life must necessarily be enhanced. This conclusion is as obviously fallacious as the former one; but impatience and unfamiliarity with the ways of others—or with the ways of the world—often lead us into it. In sum, it is the first lesson of value theory that final and instrumental values are mutually interdependent. It is feckless to project and promise intrinsic values unless we can control the necessary extrinsic values as a means to them; and it is pointless to put our labor to the procurement of instrumental values unless we also take steps to insure that these will issue in the final values that are their true ends. If I can risk a homily that is both a paraphrase and a paradox, I would state the matter thus: means without ends are altogether meaningless, while ends without means are endlessly postponed.

These remarks lead directly to the question of the conditions of value achievement. In considering this matter, the essential point to be borne in mind is that value in the strict sense is an activity or process; that is, an occurrence in human existence. It is not primarily an object, quality, situation, or ideal. Intrinsic values adhere only in those experienced occasions in which man's longings are consummated by his actions in the world. A first examination of such values as acts-in-process discloses that they have a three-fold dependence, and make a three-fold reference beyond themselves. They point backward to needs, outward to objects, and forward to fulfillments. These three dependencies constitute the basic conditions of value. If intrinsic values are to be realized, they must be animated by real needs and desires; they must find support in the resources of the world—in the physical, social, moral, and political surroundings; and they must be sustained by the requisite human energies and abilities. A brief analysis of these three conditions of value is now in order, as it should help to clarify the problems involved in social change and so to prepare us to settle the question of the proper assignment of authority.

The achievement of intrinsic values demands, in the first place, that the values in question be actively wanted and sought. Such values can never be conferred upon us by others; we must make them our own by direct and immediate participation in the process that realizes them. This process is usually arduous, always uncertain, and its fruits often long-delayed; so it is not going to be inaugurated, much less persisted in, unless people have a clear understanding and appreciation of the rewards it ultimately promises. The products, the technologies, and the institutions of high civilzation will be of no use —that is, of no instrumental value—to a society unless this society vividly anticipates and desires the way of life that these things make possible. This is the most elemental and challenging of the conditions of value, for it will always be difficult to win the enthusiasm and commitment of people to goals with which they are unfamiliar. Given this original desire and dedication, a primitive people can work miracles of improvization with the meager resources of the world and with their own untutored skills. But without this informed drive and determined engagement, expectation far outruns the possibility of attainment, promises turn into disappointments, and the value process collapses into a welter of vain hopes and shattered illusions. The gravest threats to the achivement of value—and so to successful social reform—are ignorance and apathy.

Intrinsic values are dependent, in the second place, on the resources of the world. The activities that give men satisfaction, enjoyment, and a sense of well-being are not self-sustaining: even the supposedly most self-sufficient of them—such as contemplation, worship, and love—require leisure, training, and objects upon which to be directed, while most activities stand in more obvious and pressing need of external support. The intrinsic values that we seek for ourselves—or seek to make available to others—demand access to the goods of the physical environment, such as land, tools, raw materials, food, and so forth; they demand social and political institutions that are consonant with their development and exercise; they demand appropriate educational and economic organization. Furthermore, these material conditions of value must be relevant to the goals they are meant to further and to the talents and circumstances of the people they are intended to assist. This is at once the most amenable and the most delusive of the conditions of value. It is relatively easy to supply material goods and to create educational, industrial and political establishments. It is even easier to assume that the ones we furnish will be appropriate to the needs and aspirations of people, and that they will automatically assure the procurement of intrinsic values. Our most spectacular failures in social change are probably due to our blithe acceptance of these tempting but mistaken premises.

Finally, the attainment of intrinsic values is dependent on the energies, the abilities, and the proper cultivation of the people whose values they are to be. As we have seen, intrinsic value does not lie in the mere possession of objects, the establishment of institutions, nor the achievement of position; value is not found *in* these things, but *through* them. Values reside only in experience; in man's activities and the enjoyments that accompany them. So the kinds and degree of value that men can realize are conditioned by the skills, the discipline, and the discernment that they bring with them. There are many values that require for their realization a rigorous training, a high development of latent talents, a familiarity with refined techniques, and the exercise of patience and restraint. Education, in all of its aspects, is simply preparation for value achievement. The final values that are held out to people as the fruits of social change must be commensurate with their actual powers and preparation. A people cannot be ushered into a new mode of life, as a guest into a house. This is probably the most subtle, and certainly the most onerous, of the conditions of value. It requires acute insight to measure the complex of characters that constitute a society's potentialities and its preparedness for change. Even when this is done with acceptable accuracy, the task is only begun. For it is difficult to acknowledge the ugly fact that a people cannot presently enjoy certain values because they lack the necessary skills and training. It is more difficult to announce this to the people in question. And it is all but impossible to get a people to acquiesce in this situation and to accept the postponement of what others already have and what appears so readily available. But these things must be done, for the road to revolution is paved with the disappointed promises of reform.

We can now deal rather summarily, at least in general terms, with the question of what needs to be done to assure that social reform will be effective and will in fact issue in an enhancement of life. Two broad requirements impose themselves upon this effort. In the first place, and very obviously, the values sought by reform can be achieved only to the extent that their conditions of value can be met. The way of life that is being prepared—the goals to which change is directed—must be relevant to the desires and aspirations of the people who are to live it; there must be available the necessary physical, social, and political resources to support this way of life; and the people must have the abilities, the discipline, and the training to achieve it. In the second place—and we here broach issues around which debate rages violently—the values sought by reform must be consonant with man's true nature. Peoples differ in the specific meanings that they find in such general values as freedom, beauty, love, security, participation, and so forth. And they differ in the relative importance that they attach to these values. But we still feel and act as though, underlying these differences of interpretation and emphasis, there was a broad pattern of values that commands universal allegiance. To set out to 'reform,' 'modernize,' 'improve,' or 'meliorate' a society is to assume that the changes wrought will not merely gratify the desires of its people but will yield them a higher measure of absolute value. And this in turn is to assume that we have in hand a workable, if not precise, notion of the essential potentialities of men and the mode of life that will most fully realize these. That is, we assume that human nature and human well-being are meaningful terms. However tenuous may be the philosophical footing of these ideas and ideals, they are firmly imbedded in our social and political life. Whenever we initiate or encourage social change, we pretend—and usually seriously intend—that this will enable people to lead lives that are richer in significance and satisfaction.

The essence of the problem set by these two requirements can be briefly put. Every attempted social reform is an experiment in human values. It is a question addressed to the nature of man, and it asks about the character and the conditions of the values that man seeks. As in any field of inquiry, so here we must have command of the variables with which we are dealing if we are to conduct a controlled experiment that will give us a definite answer to our question. And when we propound mistaken hypotheses, nature will here, as elsewhere, respond with a resounding 'no.' What all of this means in the present context is quite simple: if we cannot control the conditions of value, we will be unable to achieve and prove the intrinsic values that we are seeking to realize; and if we attempt to lead a people toward false or illusory values, this effort will certainly be self-defeating in the long run, whatever brief success it may have.

III

With this examination of value as a foundation and framework, we can now take up the question of the proper assignment of authority. I have argued that effective social change must be internally wrought, not externally imposed or bestowed, and that authority should therefore lie within the society that is being changed. On the basis of the preceding analysis of value, this is tantamount to claiming that elements internal to a society are in much the most favorable position to discern the intrinsic values—the goods and goals—to which this society legitimately aspires, and to understand the conditions of value that are necessary to the attainment of these goals. So my thesis now takes this form: authority must lie with elements within the society being changed, because only an authority so based can be adequately responsive to and responsible for the value claims of its people.

The first step in the argument of this thesis must obviously be a closer scrutiny of the concept of authority. The most cursory glance at this notion at once reveals two significant points. In the first place, *authority is clearly a relational term:* it is not a quality or power or condition that we attribute to anyone absolutely, as we do 'having black hair,' or 'possessing great wealth,' or 'being a violinist.' As distinct from these predications, authority can be defined and explained only as a relation between other more basic terms. Of course, common usage does speak of a person as "having authority" or being "an authority;" but such expressions are ellipses, containing implicit reference to other terms to complete their meaning. In the second place, *this relationship is triadic.* Authority is vested in rulers or governors; it is acknowledged by subjects or citizens; it is directed toward definite values or goals.

Authority can exist effectively only when all three of these elements are present: there must be rulers who are fit to wield it, subjects who are willing to accept it, and common purposes that define its uses. The relative importance of each of these factors, and so the exact relationship that holds among them, can vary in subtle and complex ways. To touch only the surface of this matter, it is at once apparent that any one of these elements may stand at the focus of the relationship and exert a dominant influence upon it. The rulers who hold authority may be so firmly entrenched—as regards the power they command, the respect they receive, and the results they achieve—that they enjoy a wide discretion in ordering the people and defining their purposes. The citizens who are subject to authority may be so jealous and suspicious of it that its use is limited, tenuous, and under constant revision. The purposes that animate and justify authority may be so desperately important and so seriously threatened that they virtually dictate what both rulers and subjects must do.

This relationship that constitutes authority is extremely volatile, and it exhibits infinite variations. But still a balance must be preserved between rulers, subjects, and purposes if authority is to be maintained. If this balance is too much disturbed, and this pattern disrupted, then authority as such vanishes, to be replaced by despotism, anarchy, or apathy. The essential point to be stressed here is that the three elements that ground this relationship are all necessary and are equally significant. Authority cannot be established on the basis of any one, or even two, of them. All must be effectively present, or the relationship collapses.

When we ask, "Who is to have authority," we immediately focus attention on only one of these elements: the rulers or governors who are to exercise authority, and whom we then tend to reify and absolutize as "the authorities." But the preceding analysis should have made it clear that this question can be adequately answered only if the other two elements that enter into the relationship are also taken into consideration. To "exercise authority" is to perform a function that is radically different from that of "wielding power" or "exerting force." It is possible to install certain individuals or groups in power, and to supply them with sufficient force to suppress opposition. But this is very certainly not to constitute them as authorities, nor does it enable them to direct a process of social reform and modernization. To fill this latter role, they must be accepted by the people who are to be subject to them, and they must be committed to purposes that are shared with this people.

This is to say that authority, like value, has its conditions. As we have just seen, the real being of authority resides in—or perhaps more exactly, it issues from—a triadic relation: it is exercised by some persons over other persons for the common attainment of value. For authority to be effectively present, each of these terms must have a satisfactory embodiment, and these embodiments must be mutually consonant. These demands impose extraordinarily difficult conditions, for they mean that each of these elements—rulers, subjects, and purposes—must be both fit for its own role and appropriate to the other two elements.

Since our present concern is to identify those who are best able to exercise authority and to direct a program of social reform, I will consider the problem posed by the conditions of authority only from that perspective. But it must be remembered that this is a dangerous, if necessary, abstraction. Those whom we call, most unfortunately, "the authorities," and whom we then come to think of as autonomous and self-sufficient, actually owe their being—their status as "in authority"—as much to their collective subjects and their society's values as to themselves. Even when the doctrine of Divine Rights was at its apogee, the position of the king was dependent upon the faith of his subjects in the providence of God. So we cannot identify the proper bearers of authority merely by considering the characteristics and capabilities of the various candidates for this role. We must also pay close attention to those over whom this authority is to be exercised and to the values that this authority is to realize—the reforms it is to institute. The character of each one of these is influenced by and varies with the characters of the other two, all three must be mutually attuned to one another, and the kind and degree of authority that is characteristic of a particular society is a function of this total relationship. We can now examine very briefly these dimensions of authority as a prelude to determining its assignment.

The internal qualifications of those who are to hold authority are obvious to the point of banality. They must be ready to make decisions, willing to accept responsibility, and able to command respect. They must be effective administrators, who can organize and manage the social effort efficiently. They must be well acquinted with the physical conditions, the institutional structures, and the human resources with which they have to work. As regards the relation between those who exercise and those who accept authorty, the essential requirement is that confidence and communication run both ways between the parties. Those in authority must have a sharp and concrete sense of what the people can and cannot do, what they will and will not tolerate, what they do and do not want. Furthermore, they must be able to present their purposes and programs in a way that is intelligible and attractive, so that they can gain the cooperation of the people. That is, rulers need to be able to form reliable and corrigible estimates of the governability of their subjects. Conversely, these latter will only acknowledge authority when they have confidence that their own needs and ambitions receive a sympathetic understanding from those who wield it. A certain amount of self-interest, favoritism, and general corruption on the part of rulers is accepted rather casually, and seems even to be expected. But those who hold authority must be able to present themselves as symbols and responsible agents of the people's aspirations. The relation between authority and its purposes—the reforms and values it is supposed to effect—is the most delicate aspect of this whole complex situation. What is here required on the part of those in authority is a fine blend of idealism and realism. They must recognize the direction and impetus of the hopes for reform that are stirring in the people; they must be able to anticipate these stirrings and to envisage them in concrete and specific terms—that is, they must be able to give imaged shape to the future. But at the same time that authority is attentive to these value claims voiced by the people, it needs to be prepared to weigh them against two criteria. It should, for one thing, measure them against those objective values that embody the accumulated experience and the refined reflection of mankind. Those vested with authority have the responsibility for criticizing and correcting the desires and ambitions of the people, not merely for fulfilling them. In the second place, authority must consider the aspirations of its people in the light of the possibilities for their accomplishment. Quite apart from what a people legitimately *should* have, what they actually and presently *can* have is dependent upon their own powers and the resources available to them.

This analysis of authority carries my argument to its climax. It was stipulated earlier that the function of authority is to direct reforms that will increase the level of value realization for the people of the society that is being reformed. So my argument has followed two lines, directed successively toward the concepts of "value" and "authority." As regards the first, I urged that intrinsic or final values consist exclusively of human activities and enjoyments. I then argued that these values can be secured only if the conditions of value can be satisfied. So authority should vest in those who can best satisfy these conditions. But our more recent inquiry has shown that authority has its own conditions, and properly belongs to those who can most fully meet them. Consequently, our original question now takes this form: Who can best fulfill the conditions of authority, and thus in turn satisfy the conditions of value, and thus, finally, direct social reforms that will promote the participation of a people in those activities and enjoyments that constitute the final values—the true ends—of life?

When the question is posed in these terms, I think there is but one answer. Authority to direct change must rest in individuals and groups who belong to the society being changed. The argument in support of this conclusion can consist only in weighing the relative capabilities of indigenous and foreign elements to satisfy the conditions of authority as these were just analyzed. And I think the outcome of such a comparison is self-evident. It is only in the first dimension of authority—that of administrative capacity—that the advantages might rest with outside experts. With respect to the second dimension—that of establishing relations of mutual confidence and communication with a native population—it is notoriously difficult for outsiders to achieve this, while local elements do it easily: in fact, they do it so easily that it sometimes constitutes a danger, for a relatively backward and suspicious people are readily gulled by their own leaders. Still, an authority that is accepted can be corrected, while a rejected authority that tries to assert itself merely intensifies resistance. But it is the third dimension—that of the relation between authority and the society's purposes—in which indigenous elements have the greatest advantage. Local leaders have a direct acquaintance with the needs, desires, aspirations, and ambitions of their people; so they are favorably placed to distinguish the licit from the illicit, and to determine both what should and what can be done. That is, they can balance idealism and realism in the reforms they institute. Elements foreign to a society lack these advantages, and when they try to exercise authority this handicap usually proves fatal. Being unfamiliar with the people and their situation, such would-be authorities cannot make a realistic appraisal of what is either desired or possible in the way of reform, nor can they project ideal goals that will be acceptable and viable. So the effort to direct social change from without usually takes one of two false paths: it either attempts to recognize and compromise all of the divergent claims voiced by the people; or it tries to impose its own vision of the Good Society and the Good Life. In short, realism degenerates toward relativism and idealism degenerates toward parochialism.

It is these considerations that dictate that authority to direct social change be vested in elements that are native to the society or group that is being changed. If this argument is in truth as persuasive as it appears to me, there is one final question that arises: Why, in the face of this evidence, do we so often persist in the effort to install foreign authority and to institute reform by outside direction? The answer I would suggest is in essence this: We do so because we confuse authority with law, and law with a body of substantive and procedural rules administered by an official personnel. This leads us to think that if we can only establish a proper legal apparatus, and staff it with duly elected or appointed officers, then the problem of authority will *ipso facto* be solved and a program of reform can be carried out. This is a gross illusion. I will discuss the matter very briefly, in a concluding section, because it will afford me the opportunity to examine the true nature and function of law in relation to authority and social change.

IV

I think that we do familiarly regard authority as a legal datum and as the creature of law. If faced with the question, common sense would probably define authority in some such terms as "legalized power," "legitimate government,' or "the right to command and be obeyed": in the language of horsemen, authority is by law out of force. But if my argument is sound, the real locus of authority is psychological, social, and moral. The primary being of authority lies in a delicate relationship between rulers, subjects, and values.

What then, one may ask, is the role of law in this matter? The answer that I will elaborate can first be stated quite simply: Law is the guise that this relationship assumes as it becomes more explicit and complex. Authority in its primordial occurrence is to a high degree personal, informal, and volatile. It is at the mercy of the idiosyncrasies of its rulers, the whims of its subjects, and the immediate purpose that these pursue; so it undergoes frequent, sudden, and radical changes. The intimacy of this primitive relationship has the advantages of sensitivity, responsiveness, and quick adaptability. But it has the corresponding disadvantages of being unstable, discontinuous, and ill-defined. So if the relationship is to endure, and particularly if it is to be capable of development, something must be done to give it a more definite form, content, and direction.

It is this need that engenders law. As societies grow in size and complexity, the authority-relationship that pervades them shifts accordingly. The exercise of authority is fractured into separate functions and shared among numerous individuals; those subject to authority segregate into limited subgroups with special interests; and the values that authority is called upon to serve become divergent and conflicting. A mode of authority that is personal and only implicit, that makes no provision for its meanings to be known until they are declared, that gives no guarantee of its future intentions and contains no assurance of the constancy of its application, is inadequate to these new conditions. What is now required is a mode of authority that is impersonal in its operations, explicit as regards its meanings and intentions, and definite in its enforcement. It is through law that authority finds the answer to these requirements. Law is the instrument through which the authority-relationship at once formalizes and concretizes itself. Authority now expresses itself as a body of purposes, principles, rules, and procedures: it designates the officials who are to administer it and the manner in which this is to be done; it assigns rights and duties, privileges and responsibilities, and so transforms rulers into governors, subjects into ctizens, and private values into the public interest and the general welfare. In sum, as authority clothes itself with law, it assumes a precise form and acquires a concrete content. Seen from this perspective, law is best described as the structural framework and operational machinery— the substantive and procedural apparatus—through which mature authority expresses and asserts itself.

Thus, far from law being the progenitor of authority, it is derivative from and dependent upon this latter. The authority-relationship between rulers, subjects, and values is the primary datum: this is the root from which law grows and which can alone sustain law in effective existence. There is of course some excuse for our persistent tendency to reverse this connection and define authority in legal terms: mistakes are rarely gratuitous. A long established and widely accepted legal system does in fact acquire a large measure of internal prestige and stability. It then comes to be acknowledged that authority belongs solely to those designated by, and is to be exercised only in accord with, legal norms. Law then appears as the natural and necessary embodiment of the authority-relationship; and it attaches to itself the moral and emotional allegiance, the habit of obedience, and the sense of purpose that constitute the heart of this relationship. Under these conditions, law becomes institutionalized, it takes on a spurious independence, and it can persist even when it is seriously distorting the relationship that originally generated it and of which it is supposedly the agent. Such a system of law can survive incompetent and corrupt rulers, discontented and divided subjects, and gross subversion of the values it is intended to guarantee.

But even in the most stable societies there is a limit to this abuse. Indeed, such societies assure their stability by express constitutional provisions for controlling the present exercise of authority by reference to its intended uses. That is, they explicitly recognize an ideal "higher law" by which actual "legal authority" can be criticized and corrected; and this "higher law" is itself an expression of the original "authority-relationship" on which the social order is based. Thus our contemporary illusion about the primacy of law is two-fold: We equate "law" with "authority" and "authority" with "the authorities." Consequently, when we set out to inaugurate programs of social reform we concentrate our efforts on drafting a legal system and designating officials to administer it.

But this, as I now hope to have shown, is to think and act at a double remove from reality. In a society that is in a nascent or revolutionary condition, authority cannot be conferred by an act in law. Quite to the contrary, acts in law, and the legal system within which they occur, are entirely dependent for their effectiveness upon the prior existence of the authority-relationship; and this relationship itself consists in a delicate and dynamic adjustment of rulers, subjects, and values. So we cannot hope to establish a legal order and institute social reform merely by drafting the personnel to carry out a preconceived program however 'constitutional' and 'representational' may be the procedures employed. This is to deal with only one element of the authority-relationship: namely, the rulers and their mode of ruling. It neglects the subjects with their antecedent allegiances and the values that give meaning to their lives. Hence it is doomed to failure.

A sound legal order is certainly an indispensable condition for effective social reform. But this legal order must itself be based upon a sound relationship between rulers, subjects, and values. Law cannot be imposed by one of these elements upon the other two. It must be the joint product of all three.

If this account of the status and function of law is correct, its meaning for our present symposium is obvious. In our efforts to establish a legal order and institute social reform we cannot look merely for those to place "in authority": this is to mistake the part for the whole. Instead, we must make the larger effort of securing a viable authority-relationship. This is to say that in asking "Who has authority?" we are posing the wrong question, so that any answer that we give must prove inadequate in principle and ineffective in practice. I think that our misadventures in many newly-independent countries —as well as our recent domestic difficulties with minority groups, organized interests, and other factions—amply confirm this diagnosis. What we need to ask is rather this: How can we modify the authority-relationship as a whole, *and the characters of its constituent elements,* in a manner to increase the yield of intrinsic value—that is, to obtain a better way of life? This is obviously a more complex question than the earlier one. So the answer will be correspondingly complex, and the process of transforming this theoretical answer into a practical solution will be slow and difficult. But at least we will be following a path that leads somewhere, instead of rushing blindly into a succession of dead-ends.

Authority and Authorization

Theodore M. Benditt

IN his book *In Defense of Anarchism*,[1] Robert Paul Wolff offers an argument designed to show that no state can be morally legitimate. His argument, roughly, is that "the defining mark of the state is authority, the right to rule" (p. 18); but, he says, the "primary obligation of man is autonomy, the refusal to be ruled." (p. 18). Since the putative authority of the state conflicts with an individual's autonomy, and since the latter is morally superior, it follows, Wolff holds, that no state has legitimate authority. The argument can be filled out as follows. A legitimate state, by definition, must have authority, or the right to rule. The correlative of the right of the state to rule is the obligation of the citizen to obey; hence, the legitimate state has a right to the obedience of its citizens. But to obey is not only to do what you have been told to do (i.e., to comply with the command), but to do this just because you have been told to do it (p. 9); "authority resides in persons." (p. 6) Thus, the legitimate state has the right to have its citizens do what it requires just because it is required, quite irrespective of the content of the requirements. However, an autonomous person could not do what someone commanded him to do just because it was commanded; he would evaluate the content of the requirement and decide for himself what he

45

ought to do. "For the autonomous man, there is no such thing, strictly speaking, as a *command*." (p. 15)

In recent replies to Wolff it has been argued that Wolff is mistaken in thinking that the correlative of the right of state to rule is the obligation of the citizen to obey;[2] that Wolff is mistaken in thinking that it is impossible for the state, just by legislating, to make something wrong that would not otherwise be wrong;[3] that Wolff confuses claims to legitimate political authority with claims to moral authority;[4] that the obligations to autonomy and authority concern different matters;[5] that Wolff fails to distinguish between state and government;[6] and others. Most of these replies to Wolff seem to me to have merit, and in what follows I do not mean to imply anything to the contrary, although despite the last mentioned objection I will continue to refer to states and not governments.

One of the arguments against Wolff is that he fails to distinguish between conclusive and prima facie obligation,[7] and that once this distinction is made, Wolff's argument is revealed to be a non sequitur. For the citizen can recognize the authority of the state by recognizing that its pronouncements (that is, those that are made in the proper way) create prima facie obligations, and this is compatible with the citizen's deciding, autonomously, that that prima facie obligation is outweighed by stronger prima facie obligations. Now let me take Wolff's part for a moment, and give a reply that the tone of his argument suggests that he might give. In what sense, one might ask, can even the legitimate state be said to be *ruling,* or to have authority, if its pronouncements are not conclusively binding on those to whom they are addressed? Just as Wolff says that "for the autonomous man, there is no such thing, strictly speaking, as a *command"* (p. 15), so he might say that if the promulgations of a legitimate state are not conclusively binding, then that state is not, strictly speaking, ruling; it does not, strictly speaking, have authority over its citizens. Thus, Wolff is (or can be taken to be) contending that if an entity is a state, then its commands are commands in the strict sense, the sense in which obedience is required and no exceptions are permissible; and if this entity is in addition morally legitimate, has the moral right to issue such commands, then, by his argument, citizens have an absolute moral obligation to obey. Wolff

agrees, however, that citizens do not have an absolute moral obligation to obey. But what this reveals, according to Wolff, is not that
there is only a prima facie obligation to obey (for such an obligation
would be incompatible with the entity's being a legitimate state having the right to *rule*), but rather that the entity in question is not
legitimate. If citizens have only a prima facie obligation to comply
with the pronouncements of the state, this cannot be grounded in the
right of the state to rule.

I would like, in what follows, to challenge the idea, implicit in
Wolff's argument and not questioned above, that a state rules, or commands, or has authority over citizens, in the strict uses of these terms.
A word about these strict uses is in order. There does seem to be a
sense, or use, of 'authority' in which a person (or group) may have
authority *over* others. In this so-called strict sense an absolute dictator
or one who held his position by divine selection (or even God himself) might say "I have (complete, absolute) authority over everyone in this nation; my word is law," where the implicaton is that if
his word were not absolutely binding on all those referred to, it would
follow that he did not have authority over them. It is this sense which
seems to be implicit in Wolff's argument; and in this sense, as I have
indicated, the distinction between absolute and prima facie obligation
does not by itself defeat his argument. My proposal is to reject
Wolff's apparent claim that an entity, if it is to be a state, must have
authority in this sense. For there can be entities that are states, in
which there is the phenomenon of authority, although they don't
rule in the strict sense or have authority over their citizens. In such
states there are individuals who are *in* authority, or who are the
authorities (not to be confused with one who is *an* authorty, on,
say, Shakespeare). Democratic states, at least, seem to be of this
sort. Our question then is how there can be authority which does not
amount to the having of absolute authority over people.

Suppose there is a small group of people trying to decide how to
go about, say, getting a governmental body to adopt a certain policy;
and suppose they succeed in reaching agreement. Since all have
agreed, each member of the group has reasons to go along with the
decision; and even if some member of the group has second thoughts,
he still has reason in that he agreed to go along, and in that the

others will be following the agreed-upon plan, so that difficulties would probably arise if some tried to go about it another way. Now let us consider a variation on the above. Suppose the group cannot reach agreement, or the individuals don't want to waste everyone's time and energy in an effort to do so; and suppose they agree to let one of their number—Brown—come up with a plan which all will follow. What we have here is a delegation of authority to Brown. Brown has the authority to decide, but not to rule in any sense; he does not have authority *over* anyone. The members of the group have an obligation to go along with his decision, but this is not a matter of obedience to Brown or to anyone else. On the other hand, the obligation does not commit us to going along if his proposal involves something decidedly immoral—as, assassination or kidnapping—as a means of accomplishing our ends, although we may not hold back just because we prefer our own solution. It is not that we have an obligation to go along which may be outweighed, but that there is no obligation at all. While we must rely here on what is implicit rather than explicit in the delegation of authority, there would seem to be no difficulty in this case in saying that such means are not part of Brown's authorization.

The foregoing shows that in an appropriate sense of 'authority,' authority and autonomy are compatible. That sense is one in which the individual in authority *has the authority to* . . . , as distinguished from the sense in which someone might have authority over others. What it is that the individual in authority has authority to do depends upon what is contained in his authorization, and the fact that a delegation of authority is not always fully detailed does not mean that what is not explicitly excluded becomes part of the authorization. We should also note that it is not the case that one who authorizes "commissions someone else to do what he himself has a right to do."[8] Some authorization is like this; for example, when a person gives a proxy, he authorizes someone to cast a vote that he himself has a right to cast. But this is not the case with our delegation of authority to Brown, for no particular authorizing individual has the right to do what he authorizes Brown to do—namely, to make a decision for the group. Nevertheless, it is clear that this is a case of authorizing someone to do something.

Our question now is how far we can push the points that have so far been developed for the case of a small voluntary group where there is at least some explicit agreement; are there any lessons here for the case of the state? We must note first that authority must be authority to do something; neither a person nor a state can have authority or be in authority without there being some acts that fall within the purview of that authority. So the compatibility of authority and autonomy depends in part upon what the purview of the authority is. In the case of our small voluntary association, the authority involved is the right of an authorized individual to make a decision as to how the group is to go about dealing with a problem; and the authority to do this, we saw, is compatible with individual autonomy. We must, then, investigate what authority there is in the state and determine whether the existence of such authority is compatible with autonomy. We must consider the following questions: What is the minimum authority that an entity can have and yet be a state? Is this authority compatible with autonomy? What authority do states typically have? Is this authority compatible with autonomy? It seems to me to be of the first importance, in considering the question of the compatibility of authority and autonomy, to bear in mind that an authorization that is limited and non-absolute[9] is still a delegation of *authority;* and the question is not whether such an authorization confers authority or not, but whether that authority is compatible wth autonomy and whether it is sufficient for there being a state.

Authority might be delegated (a) to decide how a particular problem shall be dealt with (and perhaps to deal with it); (b) to decide what problems in some given area of competence require attention (and perhaps to deal with them); (c) to decide what the areas of competence in (b) shall be; (d) to get people to act in accordance with the foregoing, where that is appropriate. Now it seems evident that authority as wide as (c)—that is, unlimited authority—can be compatible with autonomy, in the same way that authority limited to (a) in the case of our small voluntary group is compatible with autonomy. No one need be committed, by such an authorization, to immoral decisions by the authority, if the authorization can plausibly be viewed as implicitly excluding the right to make decisions which are immoral or require immoral acts. Note that such an exclusion from the authorization is compatible with authority being *unlimited;* it is not a limitation on authority, as that has been defined, for it concerns no particular area of competence or range of issues. Governments can, certainly, be authorized to legislate with respect to certain moral matters, which can constitute an area of competence or range of issues. But in this as in any area of competence governmental decisions can exceed morally allowable limits; for example, obscenity could be dealt with by setting unconscionably harsh penalties. Thus, excluding the making of immoral decisions is not just ruling out some area of competence, and is thus not a limitation on authority. And thus, to reiterate, the delegation of unlimited authority can be compatible with autonomy, for no one need be committed, by such an authorization, to any immoral decisions that the authority might make.

But since people notoriously disagree about what is or is not immoral, the question arises as to who is to determine the morality of a decision based on this authorization. If it is up to the authority to make an authoritative determination as to the morality of its decisions, autonomy is in danger. Thus, in order for unlimited authority to be compatible with autonomy, it must be the case that the authority is *not ultimate* with respect to what is moral or immoral; that is, it must not be the case that no one else has the right to review the morality of the decisions.[10] Note that this non-ultimacy of authority is of just the right sort—for not only does it mean that the decisions of the authority may fail to give rise to obligations in that they might be *ultra vires,* but at the same time they leave the citizen in a position to evaluate the morality of the decision, which is an exercise of moral autonomy. All that the decisions of an authority need give rise to is a *presumption* that one has an obligation to comply, but that presumption can be rebutted. Thus far, then, we have seen that a delegation of authority, unlimited as to subject matter or area of competence, but implicitly excluding the right to contravene morality, is compatible with autonomy.

But is such authority sufficient for a state? A delegation of authority limited to (a) would clearly not be sufficient; but one as wide as (b) begins to make the authorized entity statelike. A delegation that includes (c), even with the exclusionary provision discussed above, seems to be quite sufficient to make the authorized entity a state; and if it does, then there is no difficulty in reconciling state authority (for some possible states) with individual autonomy. States are often said to have, however, authority that extends to (d)—the right to get people to act in accordance with its decisions; and some would say further that such authority is necessary for there to be a state. Before discussing this, however, it can be observed that, whether necessary for a state or not, such authority is not incompatible with autonomy. Certainly the state's exerting force in order to produce compliance with its decisions reduces my freedom; but it does not prevent me from making an independent judgment on the moral aspects of the state's decision and from deciding what to do. And anyway it does not take away my right to do these things. Further, even my authorizing the state to use force (i.e., to limit my freedom) is not incompatible with autonomy, for the same reasons.

In any event it does not seem to be the case that there must be authority to bring about compliance, in order for there to be a state. It must, of course, be acknowledged that our picture of The Ruler or The Sovereign in a state is the picture of a strong man, one who issues edicts and commands the power, which he uses, to enforce compliance with them. In this picture one who lacks such power (or does not use it) is not in authority, for in such a situation there is non-compliance or else there is compliance with the desires or commands of others. But while this is the picture immediately conveyed by Wolff's definition of authority as "the right to command, and correlatively, the right to be obeyed" (p. 4), it is a mistake to take this as the authority required for a state. It might be risky to do without enforcement agencies; but if what such agencies accomplish were the accomplished fact without them, and without even the authorization for them, there would still remain all the authority included in (a)-(c). There is no reason to refuse to call an entity with such authority a state, for in it, *any by means of the authority delegated,* all of the other jobs can get done that need doing in any state.[11]

In conclusion, the authority of a state need not be the sort of authority that Wolff insists upon. There need not be a right to rule,

in the strict sense. Nor does there need to be a right to be obeyed, in
the sense of doing what one is told just because one is told and irrespective of what it is that he is told to do; if a state's authorization
is as I have indicated it could be, the authority of the state to decide
what is to be done is compatible with a citizen's determining for himself whether the state's decision is, from a moral standpoint, within
its authorization. Thus, at least insofar as a state can be viewed as
operating on the basis of a certain sort of authorization, it has authority, and this authority is compatible with autonomy. The argument
rests, then, on some notion of implicit delegation of authority; and
this notion has not been defended here. Many theories of implicit
delegation of authority (such as social contract, implied consent, and
others) have been offered to show that states do indeed have authority and to show what the authority is. For our purposes it has
not been necessary to defend any of these. All we need do is note
that if some theory of implicit delegation of authority to make non-
immoral decisions in all areas affecting the common good is satisfactory, then the state so commissioned has authority, and that this
authority is compatible with the autonomy of its citizens.

NOTES

1. Robert Paul Wolff, *In Defense of Anarchism* (New York: Harper,
1970). Parenthetical page references in the text are to this work.

2. Robert Ladenson, "Wolff on Legitimate Authority," *Philosophical
Studies*, v. 23 (1972), pp. 382, 383.

3. Kurt Baier, "The Justification of Governmental Authority," *Journal
of Philosophy*, v. 69 (1972), p. 712.

4. Jeffrey Reiman, *In Defense of Political Philosophy* (New York: Harper, 1972), pp. 1 ff.

5. Michael Bayles, "In Defense of Authority," *The Personalist*, v. 52
(1971), p. 758.

6. Haskell Fain, "The Idea of the State," *Nous*, v. 6 (1972), p. 21.

7. Stanley Bates, "Authority and Autonomy," *Journal of Philosophy*, v.
69 (1972), p. 178; and Bayles, *op. cit.*, pp. 755-6.

8. R. S. Peters, "Authority," *Political Philosophy*, ed. A. Quinton (New
York: Oxford University Press, 1967), p. 86.

9. "First, absolute authority is based on an absolute rather than *prima
facie* obligation to obey; that is, no other obligations can override that of

obedience. Second, unlimited authority contrasts with limited authority. The distinction concerns the range of issues over which an authority governs." (Bayles, *op. cit.*, p. 756).

10. This formulation of nonultimacy of authority is adapted from Bayles, *op. cit.*, p. 756: "Third, authority is ultimate if the decisions made by a person or group of persons having it cannot be reversed or invalidated by another authority."

11. A. D. Woozley. in "The Existence of Rules," *Nous,* v. 1 (1967), pp. 76ff., maintains that laws need not be enforceable in order to exist, or in order for a legal system to exist; they need only be "operable." "A law is operable to the extent that there is no risk of successful defiance to it. One way, but not the only way, of achieving this end is to have an effective enforcement agency, to secure the failure of defiance. Another way is to have no risk of defiance, as, for example, where the party concerned has sufficient respect for the authority concerned, or for the rule of law, or for the weight of adverse opinion." (p. 78)

On the Justification
of Political Authority

Rex Martin

THE notion of political authority and the logic of its justification are intimately tied in with the concept of the state. This connection is useful for our purposes, for *state* is widely used as a descriptive term and, indeed, has been given a degree of technical precision by political scientists. We are aware, of course, that the technical sense captures only the idea of a *de facto* state; nonetheless, it should be possible to construct a *de jure* conception on this foundation.

First, however, we should note an equivocation in the term *state*, namely, that it can refer either to a politically organized society or to an agency for making laws, and so on, in that society. There is no philosophical advantage in deciding which of these references is the proper one. Whether one takes the term *state* to refer to a politically organized society or to a government, the same problem remains: What is involved for that thing to be a state? In order to avoid the equivocation, though, I would suggest use of two distinct terms: *polity* (to refer to a politically organized society) and *government* (to refer to an agency for making laws, and so on).

Now we are ready, I think, to consider a preliminary working definition: "A polity is a politically organized society. A society is political, or has a government, if it contains a determinate agency (or correlated set of agencies) to formulate, apply, and enforce commands for all the people in that society; if these commands are

54

generally obeyed (that is, usually and by most people); and if the agency itself has a monopoly *in principle* of the use of physical force for coercion, at least in the sense that it forbids, more or less successfully, the use of such force on the part of the citizens."

As I have already indicated, this definition is intended principally as an "empirical" one, that is, it is meant to cover instances at different times in history and it is supposed to be in accord with ordinary usage, again from various cultural and historical periods. It is a successful definition to the extent that it allows us to say that Plato, Aquinas, and Locke were all talking about 'the state,' even though we are aware that they probably had widely different things in mind when they used the words that we translate as "state." Moreover, it should enable us to accommodate the differences that exist between, say, a modern territorial state with sovereign power, a medieval kingdom, a Greek polis, and a seminomadic tribe. And it should allow us to differentiate between a polity and a society that has no government or between a polity and a mere association (like a university or a club) or between a polity and a church.

The usual way in which we would distinguish a polity from a voluntary group or a church, even a church as powerful as the one that existed in the Middle Ages, is by stressing the notion that a government has a monopoly in the use of physical force. A government characteristically uses force, or threatens to, as a way of backing up its rules and commands. Thus, Thoreau said that when he was released after his one night in jail he "joined a huckleberry party"; in half an hour they had gotten to the huckleberry field "on one of our highest hills, two miles off," and he added significantly, "then the State was nowhere to be seen." In short, states or polities are different from such things as huckleberry picking parties and the difference largely comes down to a matter of courts and jails.

All of this is rather standard fare. We normally adopt the distinction I have indicated, thereby emphasizing the element of physical coercion, when we are called upon to distinguish the social from the political sphere. We could simply say, then, that there is an intrinsic connection between being a government and using or threatening physical force. Accordingly, to say that a government has rightful or legitimate authority is to say that it could *by right* back up its laws with force and employ this force against lawbreakers. Here, then, the justification of *political* authority would be the justification for a government's forbidding, or being in a position to forbid, the use of coercive force to its subjects while maintaining coercion and the threat of coercing on its own behalf. And the logic of justifying political authority would amount to the logic of justifying the possession by a government of precisely this sort of coercive power.

We are now able to make a distinction between *de facto* and *de jure* political authority. We can do so by setting alongside our earlier "empirical" definition a definition in "normative" form. And this normative form can be achieved simply by adding a word to the "empirical" definition, thereby amending it to read that the political agency itself has "a *rightful* monopoly . . . of the use of physical force. . . ."

But, surely, in saying this we want to suggest also that the political agency is somehow entitled to issue commands or rules in the first place. It would be unreasonable to say that a government has a title to back up its decrees with threats and even the use of force without saying at the same time that it has a rightful license to issue these rules. So, there are really two things involved here: the license to issue certain rules and a possible title to enforce them coercively.

Moreover, it would appear to be self-contradictory to say that a government has a rightful capacity to prohibit *all* use of force to its subjects while denying that it had a rightful title to issue any rules at all. For it could be replied that a capacity to *prohibit* by right requires and would involve a title to issue prohibitive *rules*. Accordingly, it would seem that the introduction of the notion of a *rightful* monopoly in the use of physical force into our "normative" definition also requires the introduction of the notion of a determinate agency have a *rightful* license to formulate and issue commands.

It would follow on this analysis that the authority of a government principally resides in the notion that it can and does formulate laws enabling it to prohibit force to its subjects or to use it to enforce its own rules. But we have not yet provided a ground for these rules to be obeyed; we have not, up to now, provided for any reasonable expectation of general compliance.

One could say that this is provided for by the coercive element in our analysis. People would obey, or we could reasonably expect them to, because they do not want to be penalized; they obey because they are forced to. But if we added a normative component to the very idea of obeying, if we said, for example, that the reasonable expectation of general compliance was a rightful one, then it is not clear that this answer would do. People might obey because they feared to do otherwise, but that they *ought* to obey *in any case* raises a wholly different issue.

There is still a kind of hiatus in our account of authority. We can connect the title to enforce rules with the title to issue them and the capacity to prohibit subjects from using force with the license to issue rules. But we cannot as yet bring in an *obligation* to obey the rules. We have failed to make our "empirical' definition wholly normative, for we cannot connect the normative capacity of the government in its monopoly of the use of force with any *normative* expectation of general compliance.

I think a similar defect would plague us were we to start with a rightful presumption of compliance. We could, perhaps, move from there to an original title to issue rules or commands; but it is not clear that we could take a further required step. For if one started with the claim that these commands *ought* generally to to obeyed, it would not necessarily follow that such commands should be coercively enforced in the absence of compliance.

The notion of the state has three main parts: the issuing of rules, the expectation of general compliance, and the possession by government of a monopoly in the use of coercive force. And, if my claim is sound that the notion of political authority is to be mapped onto that of the state, it would follow that the notion of political authority has these same three parts. Where that notion is made normative, as it would be in the idea of a *justified* political authority, the same three elements are still present. Hence, the logic of justifying political authority must be a logic of exhibiting a connection between these three elements in their normative form.

The notion of a justified political authority is a systematic one and the logic of its justification must involve establishing systematic connections. What we have to show, then, is that a rightful license to

issue rules does connect with a rightful presumption of compliance
and that such a connection does confer a possible title to back up
these rules coercively.

At this point it might be contended that I have been alleging
a problem in relating two notions—the rightful license to issue rules
and the obligation to obey them—but that no such problem exists.
The two notions are already connected, in virtue of their meaning,
and the problem vanishes simply in seeing this. This is a persuasive
reply and has considerable vogue among contemporary political
philosophers; hence it might be worth examining at some length.
Even so, it will not allow us to dispense with both features of the
problem I have raised, for there remains the question of a connection
between the rules-issuing license and the citizen's obligation to obey,
on the one hand, and the coercive enforcement of these rules, on the
other. But I will turn to that matter only after I have first dealt with
the linkage between rule issuing and obligation.

Many contemporary political philosophers, as I have indicated,
see a close connection between the rule-issuing authority of government and the obligation of the citizen. It is, indeed, an analytic connection. To say that a government has such authority means, or entails, that every citizen has an obligation to obey its particular laws.
For example, D. D. Raphael says, "The authority of the State implies
that those who exercise it have the right (of action) to issue
orders and the right (of recipience) to have those orders obeyed, and
that, corresponding to the second right, the citizens have a duty or
obligation to obey the orders" (*Problems of Political Philosophy*
[London: Pall Mall Press, 1970], p. 78; see also pp. 68-69, 72-74).
A conventional political philosopher like Raphael is not alone in
thinking this; many defenders of the anarchist point of view hold the
connection to exist, as an analytic one, as well. For example, we find
Robert Paul Wolff saying that legitimate authority is "a matter of
the *right* to command, and of the correlative obligation *to obey the
person who issues the command.* . . . It is a matter of doing what he
tells you to do *because he tells you to do it*" (*Defense of Anarchism*
[New York: Harper and Row Torchbooks, 1970], p. 9; see also pp.
4-5, 40) .

Even philosophers who are not defenders of the anarchist or of the statist viewpoint and who would claim to restrict themselves to conceptual analysis endorse the notion of a connection of entailment between rule-issuing authority and obligation. For instance, Thomas McPherson says, "Now, to hold that some person or some body has authority is to hold that he or it ought to be obeyed. This, again, is part of what we mean by 'authority' ... " (*Political Obligation* [London: Routledge and Kegan Paul, 1967], p. 59; see also pp. 60-62 and 64-65).

Accordingly, since it is believed that this tight entailment connection holds, the anarchist undertakes to deny political obligation by denying political authority, but what he means by "authority" is "that which requires obligation," and the statist undertakes to affirm political authority by affirming political obligation. They occupy a common ground. As Wolff put it, "The normative concept of the state as the human community which possesses rightful authority [that is, the rule-issuing authority correlated with the citizens obligation to obey] thus defines the subject matter of political philosophy proper" (*Defense of Anarchism*, p. 11). The fundamental point is that both parties to the dispute resolve the issue of a rule-issuing *authority* into that of the citizen's strict *obligation* to obey the rules issued.

Hence, the logic of justifying political authority for each reduces to the single crucial consideration that a government has authority to issue rules if and only if citizens have a strict obligation to obey those rules. The anarchist and the statist differ, then, only in that one denies and the other affiirms this strict obligation. But each is committed to the view that political obligation is the logically prior issue.

The dispute between the anarchist and statist comes down to the issue of whether the citizen is strictly bound to obey all laws just insofar as they are laws. The essence of what is at issue, as I see it, is the notion that citizens have a *special* obligation towards laws as such, as distinct from an obligation to do a certain thing whether it is prescribed by law or not. The nature of this obligation is that one is to do what he is told to do simply because it is mandated by law. The obligation is a strict one; it attaches to all laws and can be overridden, if at all, only in exceptional cases.

I think the Socrates of Plato's *Crito* held something very like this view, and held it in a particularly strong and uncompromising version.[1] Kant, too, was a political obligationist. Unlike Socrates, who espoused a doctrine of unmitigated obligation, Kant held that the obligation to obey the law could be overridden only if what the law commanded was immoral.[2] The position of most political obligationists is more akin to that of Kant than to Socrates in that they regard political obligation as strict but possible of mitigation.

Hobbes, who is often thought to hold the doctrine of an absolute obligation to obey, actually allowed that a matter of life or death could exempt the citizen, even the citizen under criminal penalty, from the obligation to obey.[3] And Locke, who sounds like an uncompromising absolutist when he lays down his doctrine of civil obligation on the basis of his contract theory, limts the obligation significantly in his subsequent discussion of the so-called right of revolution.[4] The examples suggest that the obligationist view has been a fairly common one in the history of political philosophy and that the dispute between the philosophical anarchist and the statist is deeply embedded there.

Now if political obligation is not thought to be derived from the notion of authority, it must be grounded in some other way. And since obligation is the *prior* question in the perspective under discussion, we cannot start by positing authority. Rather, we must go outside the political system, outside the idea of the state, to find the ground of political obligation. We must look for an obligation-conferring trait *external* to the body politic and bring that to bear on the issue of the citizen's standing before the law.

For example, one could allege that a person has a standing of obligation towards the laws if it is divinely commanded that men obey laws, that is, obey laws simply because they are laws. Or, again, the man who has bound himself to obedience by an oath or some sort of promise would have an external ground of obligation to obey all particular laws.

We can, of course, imagine a mixed case where the "contract" of obedience was intrinsic to a system of politics and where, on the basis of that "contract," one was alleged to have a strict obligation to obey laws. The "contract," which both authorizes government to make laws and binds the contracting parties to strict obedience, is an integral feature of a system of politics. But it is also conceived to be a "contract," and it governs the obligation just as *any* contract would whatever its nature or whoever the contracting parties are. Here, apparently, we have a mixed case.

I doubt, though, that this appearance is conclusive. The essential question is whether the citizen's obligation to law derives from his being a party to a contract (note the parallel case of Socrates' having made an agreement with the Laws to obey them). If it is indeed the contractual relationship that grounds the obligation then, clearly, obligation is here conceived as externally grounded. The test, then, is always to ask: How is the obligation to obey laws thought to be grounded? And it is evident that in many theories the relationship of citizens to the government is construed as a case of some nonpolitical undertaking, like promising or signing a contract, which is obligation-creating in character.

I would argue that an external ground of political obligation never creates a strict obligation to obey laws as such. When God commands us to obey all laws, we obey them because God says so. Our obligation is to what God commands and not principally to the laws at all. Nothing about law itself or about the system of political concepts, without the superaddition of the will of God, makes obeying laws obligatory.

Similarly, when utility commands us to obey all laws, we obey them because it is useful to the end of the greatest happiness of the greatest number. Our obligation is, logically, to the principle of utility; our obligation to subordinate rules or "findings" holds only insofar as they accord with it. Again, there is nothing about law, except under the superordinate principle of utility, that makes obedience obligatory.

If this point were insisted upon by a utilitarian and if he were, further, to assert that the subordinate "rules"—such as "obey the law"—under the utilitarian principle are nothing but rule-of-thumb maxims based on the experience that following the rule in question usually results in a "good" outcome, then he would be in a position to say that we are never under a *strict* obligation to obey laws. This is, I think, one basis for the philosophical anarchism of Godwin, who was a utilitarian.[5]

Further, the logic of Wolff's main argument in defense of anarchism is captured in the account I have given of these external grounds of political obligation. Instead of the will of God, or of the demands of act-utilitarian justice, Wolff posits the absolute moral and intellectual autonomy of the individual as the external ground. Since this postulate of autonomy is a moral "demand" (see *Defense of Anarchism*, pp. 17 and 72),Wolff's position is more like Godwin's than like, say, William of Occam's.[6]

It is in this context that I would like to set Wolff's allegation of a "genuine incompatibility" between political authority and individual autonomy.[7] Wolff's point, I take it, is that if individual persons are under the sovereign and permanent "demand" of moral and intellectual autonomy, then they can never be under an obligation to do what they are commanded to do simply because it is mandated by law. There is no obligation that attaches to laws *as a rule,* hence no strict obligation to do whatever the law says.

But I don't think there is advantage in pursuing Wolff's general line of argument further. It is one instance of a general type. True, there may be marginal, even important, differences within the type. For example, unlike the divine will as external ground, which does allow that we can be obligated by God to obey man-made laws, Wolff's position rules out altogether any obligation to obey laws for an autonomous man. But all the external ground analyses, each for its own reason, rule out the notion of a special obligation to laws as laws. And this, I think, is the crucial consideration.

All these analyses, whether they draw the anarchist conclusion or not, follow the same logical pattern. (a) A tight connection is assumed between political authority, in the rule-issuing sense, and political obligation. (b) The issue of justifying political authority is, accordingly, reduced to the question whether citizens have a strict obligation to obey laws just insofar as they are valid laws. (c) Since obligation is given priority here, the justification of strict political obligation is made the central issue and the question of the justification of political authority is thought to turn on it. (d) But since obligation is logically prior to all the other political concepts, the task of justifying it requires that we go outside the whole system of political concepts. (e) Hence the justification, whether it can be accomplished or not, must be attempted by reference to some external, non-political standard .

But the very procedure of justification here creates a deep conceptual problem. As we have seen, the only ground for a *strict* obligation to obey law must lie in some politically external standard. But to repair to this standard, as the logic of the justificatory scheme requires, is to treat these obligations as non-politically derived. Hence, all external grounds exclude *political* obligation, that is, special obligations to obey laws *qua* laws, in principle. It follows, then, either that we may have obligations to the law but these can never be strict ones or that none of the strict obligations we may have can be obligations to the laws *per se*. We are left with only one conclusion: *that we can have no strict political obligations at all.*

It is the perception of this fact that has been seized upon by the philosophical anarchist. But his claim that where we have external grounds of obligation we have no *political* obligations is merely a redescription of the contention that our standing before the law is governed by external grounds of obligation. Nonetheless, his strictures are telling against traditional external justifications of political authority which rely on grounding that authority in the citizens' strict obligation to obey the laws issued. For these accounts are subject to the conceptual pressures generated by their own justificatory scheme. And since they share that scheme with the anarchist, they can never free themselves from the toils of his argument.

Now one might be tempted to solve this problem by a simple expedient: Simply *reverse* the priorities involved, putting political authority ahead of political obligation. Indeed, this style of analysis represents another common pattern in political philosophy.

Consider, for instance, the case of St. Paul. His famous letter to the church of Rome speaks of "being subject," but the degree to which Christian subjection involved any real commitment to obey law is not clear. (See *Romans* xiii, 1-7.) In any event, whether the apostolic counsel was an obligationist one or not, it was rigorously governed by the consideration that we ought to "obey God rather than men" (*Acts* v, 29) in cases of conflict. And this judgment, in its turn, was based on a prior determination of authority or, to speak more precisely, on a prior judgment as to the precedence of one level (or type) of authority over another. For, as can readily be seen, Paul based his counsel to "be subject" on a doctrine of authority: "Let every person be subject to the governing authorities. For there is no authority except from God, and those that exist have been instituted by God" (*Romans* xiii, 1).

No doubt the martyrdom of Peter and Paul at the hands of the Roman state indicates the clear perception they had of the priority of "authorities" and of the subordination of the authority of the state to that of the divine will. And if they were obligationists respecting the law, they were extraordinarily clear-headed in their conception of that doctrine.

It should be obvious, however, that the move to make political authority conceptually prior to political obligation cannot solve the problem I have identified. For, if the ground on which political authority is to be justified is itself politically ulterior (as it is in the case of resorting to the divine will or of using the analogy of parental authority over young children), nothing *political* grounds the justification.

Whatever the ground for justifying political authority here is, it is not a ground within, not an integral feature of any theoretic system of political concepts. Authority proper attaches, not to the law-making role or the system of concepts in which it is embedded, but to the external ground. The political system and that which could confer authority on it are, necessarily, separated conceptually.

This is all that the philosophical anarchist would need to make his case. For he could, in the same way that he argued against political obligation, always provide an external ground for rejecting political *authority*. By saying that the notion of political authority, although a coherent one, is subordinate to some extrinsic notion he could "remove" it on that basis.

This capacity of anarchism, however, represents not so much the peculiar vulnerability of political authority to critique as it does the exploitation by the anarchist of inherent defects in the externalist program for justifying political authority. But locating these defects is another matter. As I have already indicated, I do not think the

defect lies in making political obligation the prior concept over political authority rather than the other way around. For the problem
remains under either option. Nor does the defect lie in the requirement that the citizens' obligation to obey the law be a *strict* one. Even
if that requirement were to be relaxed, as it is in theories of civil disobedience, the obligation would still be *externally* grounded and to
that extent it would not be an obligation towards the laws just as
laws.[8]

Perhaps, though, the defect does lie close to the things we have
just mentioned. Perhaps the problem is with the very notion of making either obligation or authority the *prior* concept.

The externalist program for justifying political authority requires
that we take *one* element in the idea of political authority, say, the
license to issue rules or the reasonable expectation of compliance,
and lift it clean out of the theoretic system of political concepts to
bring it under some external normative standard, such as the divine
will or an ultimate ethical principle (like that of utility). Hence, the
externalist program commits us to a piecemeal treatment of the notion of political authority, whereby we remove elements of that
notion from a particular system in which they are located and in so
doing sunder the connections that this element has within that system to the other ingredient elements in the notion of authority.

The externalist program, in short, makes it impossible to exhibit
the systematic connections which render the notion of political authority distinctively a notion of *political* authority. Rather, it removes
some element of the notion and moralizes it, or baptizes it; but what
it takes out of the system, no longer having its systematic connections
and its place there, is no longer characteristically *political*.

For example, the obligation to obey the law is not treated in the
accounts we have examined as a *political* obligation. On the contrary, it is treated exclusively as a *moral* one, or as a divinely commanded one, and it takes its place, if it has one, in a list of Moral
Rules, on a par with the obligation to keep promises, or in an abstract heaven of Divine Commandments.[9] The defect of the externalist program is that it makes it systematically impossible to ask
whether the peculiar *political* standing that a citizen has before the
law is one that can be morally approved. For it is never determined,

and given the externalist program, never could be, that such an obligation is *inherent* in the citizen's standing before the law in a system determined by a given set of political concepts.

The solution to the problem, though, seems ready at hand. Rather than take *one* of the elements in the idea of political authority—be it the title to issue rules or the reasonable presumption of compliance or the government's rightful monopoly in the use of coercive force—and lift it out for inspection under the light of some external source of authority, we might try to work up the elements together. Or, better, we might try to work up a theoretic system of political concepts in which all these elements would be ingredient. Here, in contrast to the externalist program for justifying political authority, is the germ of an alternative scheme: a program for an *internal* justification of political authority.

As I see it, the question of political authority, whether it is an intrinsic feature in a theoretic system of political concepts or not, really depends on what that system is. Hence, to see whether different systems really can support a notion of political authority we would need to give body to the different notions that make up first one theoretic system of political concepts and then another.

In concluding my argument I want to sketch out one example of an *internal* justification of political authority. In order to do this I will construct, schematically, a particular political system. I want to show in doing this only how political authority could be justified there; I will not actually attempt to "do" the fullscale justification in this paper.

Let us imagine a theoretic schema for a political system which would include at a minimum such notions as civil rights and democratic electoral procedures. We can specify further that civil rights are legal rights of the following character: (a) they are rights of all persons, all subjects, in that society; (b) they are, presumptively, part of the "good" of each person or instrumental to it; (c) they identify ways of acting, or ways of being acted toward, which would be claimed by each person for himself as well as for all the others in that society.

In other words, a particular line of conduct, or of forebearance, is agreed upon because it is in the interest of each and all the members:

each claims it for himself and recognizes it for all the others. A way of acting so secured is a right and when secured by recognition in law it is a civil right.

I think it arguable, whatever one might think about so-called natural or human rights, that *civil* rights require stating. They must be issued by some body. Moreover, they must be applied, at least in the sense of being given some determinate content and, then, lived up to. And, where rights conflict, they must be harmonized. When we have rights, issued and applied and coordinated, we have a *system of rights*. And we could not have such a system without agencies to do those things and these, in turn, would have to exhibit some degree of coordination themselves. Here, then, government would enter the picture as instrumental in the production of rights.

But how could these agencies be presumed to issue rights-rules, specifications of ways of acting, that *were* in the interest of each subject or that, arguably, would be claimed by each of them as a universal rule? This is a hard question, but one might answer that this is where the democracy part comes in. Having democratic procedures available doesn't assure that the right-rules issued will have the character claimed. But we can at least *presume,* a refutable presumption in the individual instance, that they would.

The reason these electoral and parliamentary procedures would tend to be productive of rights is found in those very features which allow us to characterize the process as a democratic one in the first place. The institutions of a democratic policy do put great emphasis on such matters as regular elections, freedom to campaign and vote, and majority—or plurality—rule by means of representative bodies and established procedures. But the important point here is not the fact of majority rule alone but, rather, the fact that each citizen is to count for one and no more than one in the determination of that majority. Citizens come from all walks of life, differing in race, place of origin, religion, gender, social class, occupation, educational background, income, ethnic affinity, lifestyle; yet they are counted in the tabulation of votes simply as citizens. Democratic institutions not only represent this plurality of citizens but must also appeal to it for their foundation and constantly create these pluralities anew. Accordingly, when we have rules produced in conformity to demo-

cratic procedural norms we can have some assurance that many people, including representative persons from all walks of life, have
affirmed, or would affirm, these rules.

I would not want to deny that there are features of any society,
other than its being democratic, that might work against the production of rights; my point is simply that the democratic features do,
characteristically, conduce towards the end in question, that of producing rights. Moreover, I would not want to leave the factor of time
and experience out of the picture. Sometimes rights-rules do not
meet with widespread favor and their initial effect may be somewhat
divisive socially, but if they really are rules specifying *rights,* time
and experience will tell in their favor and the degree of social
approval and the identification of one's own interest and of the interest of society in such rules will grow extensively over the years.
This has certainly been true of the American experience in such
matters as the abolition of slavery and the ending of racial segrega-
tion in many of its aspects. Hence, I would argue that we can presume a decided tendency for democratic procedures, taken on their
own and over time, to be productive of civil rights.

Now, of course, this presumption would probably not hold if
the majority did whatever it wanted, whenever it wanted to. But
if the majority always takes as its object the production of rights-
rules or, at least, the issuance of no rules incompatible with existing
rights-rules, then the presumpton I have identified could hold *as a
presumption.*

So we see that civil rights-rules do require an agency or set of
agencies to issue and apply them. And we see that agencies based on
democratic procedures, if they dedicated themselves to producing
civil rights-rules, would presumptively be able to issue just such
rules. Since this presumption is measurably weaker with any non-
democratic form of government, there seems to be a conceptual affinity between the idea of civil rights and that of democratic electoral
procedures. They are connected and, accordingly, the idea of a system
of rights would have both these elements in it.

Now it might be alleged that good citizenship in a rights-produc-
ing polity, one where presumptive civil rights-rules were produced on
a democratic electoral basis, involves some sort of strict commitment

to abide by the laws that define these rights. I do not want to pass judgment on this allegation, but one can at least see the point of its being made; one can see how it might arise within the idea of a system of rights for anyone who was thinking seriously about that system.

At issue here is whether the idea of a system of rights requires *strict* compliance by the citizens with its laws, at least with those that are civil rights laws. Moreover, even if we should decide *against* the citizen's obligation of *strict* compliance, the limitations inherent in any such decision should be noted. For whatever the standing of the citizens towards the law is, it is a special one, one that attaches to the laws as such. We might describe it, briefly and in a general way, as a presumptive bond of compliance. When the citizen act so as to conform to law he does so, at least in part, simply because a certain line of conduct has been mandated by law. He need not, of course, do it in an automatic and unthinking manner; he can even hold in reserve a decision *not* to comply on occasion.

There is then, surely, no question that good citizenship in a system of rights would involve compliance, generally, with civil rights laws. But if the compliance was not *required* to be strict, we could allow for the possibility of civil disobedience. Indeed, the idea of consent built into both the notion of civil rights and the notion of democratic electoral procedures might even *require,* conceivably, some cases of civil disobedience—where, for example, the citizen regarded an alleged rights law as positively inimical to his own interest and to the interest of many of those subject to it and hence, as specifying a way of acting that he could not endorse.

Perhaps I can put my point more simply. In this system, obedience may not attach to all laws as a rule, allowing only for well founded and narrowly prescribed exceptions. Rather, what might attach as a rule is *civilly* responsible and appropriate conduct. Here there would be no rule mandating obedience to law and, hence, no exception to that rule. In a system of rights, *strict* political obligation, where obedience is either an unfailing rule (Socrates) or an unfailing one in a legitimate state (Locke) or an unfailing one except in a case of life or death (Hobbes), may not even exist.

So we see that when we talk about the citizen's obligation to obey laws or about civil disobedience, it is very important to have a particular kind of state in mind. For some kinds of state can "take" civil disobedience and even incorporate it as a feature of their theoretic structure. But other kinds are *logically* incapable of doing this; the concept, the theoretic structure of such states won't allow it. This would suggest that something weaker than strict obligation is compatible with the notion of a rule-issuing authority. Accordingly, we might mark this point by discarding the idea of a relationship of strict entailment between rule-issuing authority and the obligation to obey those rules. And in place of obligation we might put the notion of *allegiance,* on the principle that for any given theoretic system of political concepts there is correlated to the rule-issuing authority in that system an appropriate allegiance on the part of citizens, some peculiar standing of the citizens towards the laws issued in that system.[10] Hence the kind of state, the exact nature of the theoretic system of political concepts 'for that particular state, would become the crucial question.

In this brief sketch I have indicated how two of the elements in the traditional notion of political authority—the title to issue rules and a reasonable expectation of compliance with these rules—can be regarded as ingredient in a particular theoretic system of political concepts, in the illustration used, a system of rights. Even so, it should not be a foregone conclusion that a political agency which has a justified title to issue rules and to require compliance thereby has the title to punish, that is, the right to attach penalty clauses to its laws and to enact penalties against lawbreakers. The matter is more complex than that.

I would argue that punishment, as a political-legal practice, is itself always located in a particular political system and that it must be justified by reference to its "system-located aim" or "function." Hence, to justify punishment is to display its rationale, to show its place, and the "necessity" for it there, within a particular system of political institutions and principles. I do think it worth observing, however, that punishment would be *prima facie* justified in the particular political system we have been concerned with, a system of rights, if (1) it would help maintain the condition of non-interference with determinate rights and (2) if it was necessary either because no alternative way would do the job or because no alternative way could do the job as well.

We see, then, how it might be possible to extend our analysis of a system of rights to include an internally justified practice of punishment in it. Whether we could take the matter one step further, to include the government's prohibition of the use of force, in principle *all* use of force, by its subjects, is not clear. It does seem that a use of force which was violative of determinate rights could justifiably be prohibited. Hence, we at least have a criterion for deciding the issue and it is a powerful criterion since, in principle, it would be possible to prohibit *all* use of force by ordinary citizens on the basis it provides.

It seems, accordingly, that if my sketch could be filled in, these conclusions sustained, and the connections they involve amplified, we would have a clear idea of what is involved in the internal justification of political authority respecting at least one political system. I realize that if a different system had been chosen, a different analysis, and perhaps different conclusions, would have been required. Even so, I think the basic logical points involved here would be invariant for all such systems.

There is, in particular, an interesting connection between the externalist scheme for justifying political authority and what I have called an internal justification of that authority. The external scheme requires that we bring political authority under some politically ulterior standard. But in order to do this the externalist scheme requires the very internal justificatory procedure I have been describing. For without first establishing that political authority is both a *political* and a *justified* authority, the externalist program seems to have little point. However, once the internal justification is completed, the externalist is in a position to ask an important question. He can ask whether a given theoretic system of political concepts, in which the elements of authority have been established as ingredient, can be morally approved. This is the same as asking whether political authority can be morally justified.

In short, I think the externalist program for justifying political authority is one step removed from where it is normally thought to operate. Rather than deal with the question of justifying *political* authority, it is peculiarly suited to raise the question whether an authority that is politically justified can be *morally* justified. For if there is such a thing as an independent moral justification of political authority, it is probably at the level of justifying an entire political system and, hence, can be a justification of *political* authority only in virtue of a prior internal justification.

Similarly, the pattern of justification I am discussing would entail certain changes in the strategies of philosophical anarchism. For on the analysis I have developed, the characteristic device of the philosophical anarchist, to remove political authority simply on external grounds, would be a category mistake, since the notion of *political* authority is an intrinsic one, belonging always to a particular theoretic system of political concepts.

The philosophical anarchist could, of course, carry his fight right into the system of political concepts. Although it would be difficult to do, it is possible that he could establish an internal case for rejecting the notion of political authority, at least in the sense of a government's having the title to coerce. The philosophical anarchist might even succeed in indicating the problematic character of all theories of authority, or even of the very notion of political authority.

To do any of these things, towards the end either of justifying political authority morally or of denying it in the manner of the philosophical anarchist, one must begin by attempting to establish or justify authority with respect to the other notions that constitute a particular theoretic system of political concepts. To this extent, then, the program for an internal justification of political authority is logically unescapable.[11]

NOTES

1. I am talking specifically of Socrates' arguments in the *Crito*. For those interested in the details of Socrates' arguments against disobedience to law, I would suggest a reading of that part of the *Crito* which deals with "Socrates' Dialogue with the Personified Laws of Athens." (See Plato, *Euthyphro, Apology, Crito,* tr. F. S. Church [2d ed; New York: Library of Liberal Arts, 1956], pp. 60–65.) I have argued elsewhere that Socrates should be taken as saying that, where a man cannot dissuade the authors of the law from putting it into effect, then he *must* obey the law. (See "Socrates on Disobedience to Law," *Review of Metaphysics* XXIV.1 [September 1970],

21–38). Some writers, of course, have rejected the view that Socrates advocates an absolute obligation to obey the law. They do so largely by drawing on statements made by Socrates in Plato's *Apology*. The best essays in defense of this position are A. D. Woozley's "Socrates on Disobeying the Law" in G. Vlastos (ed.), *The Philosophy of Socrates: A Collection of Critical Essays* (Garden City, N. Y.: Doubleday Anchor Books, 1971), pp. 299–318, and F. C. Wade, "In Defense of Socrates," *Review of Metaphysics* XXV.2 (December 1971), 311–25. The discussion of Socrates' position has begun, of late, to grow into a literature of some proportion. Among the more recent pieces, the essay by G. G. James, "Socrates on Civil Disobedence and Rebellion," *Southern Journal of Philosophy* XI.1 and 2 (Spring and Summer 1973), 119–127, might prove helpful.

2. "Obey the authority which has power over you (in everything which is not opposed to morality) is a categorical imperative" (W. Hastie [tr.], *Kant's Philosophy of Law* [Edinburgh: T. & T. Clark, 1887], p. 256). That Kant took his dictum quite seriously is attested to by his own conduct. In 1794, he was rebuked by the monarch for his *Religion Within the Bounds of Reason Alone* and was enjoined to discontinue publication on this subject. Kant assured the King of the honesty of his motives and of his conscience but, nonetheless, complied: "as Your Majesty's most loyal subject, I will abstain in lectures or in writing. . . . " He had earlier said in a letter, "If new laws order me to do what is not against my principles, I will precisely obey them." He said, also, "But to be silent in a case like the present is the duty of a subject." (All three quotes came from A. D. Lindsay, *Kant* [London: E. Benn, 1934], p. 12.) The reader might want to consult on this point the interesting essay "The Sweet Dream: Kant and the Revolutionary Hope for Utopia" by Melvin J. Lasky in *Encounter* XXXIII. 4 (October, 1969), 14–27.

3. The subject's "right" here is neither moral nor political but a "right of nature," the right of self-preservation. (See T. Hobbes, *Leviathan,* ed. M. Oakeshott [Oxford: Basil Blackwell, 1957], chap. 21, pp. 141–43.)

4. Locke asserts a strict obligationist position: "And thus every Man, by consenting with others to make one Body Politick under one Government, puts himself under an Obligation to everyone of that Society, to submit to the determination of the *majority,* and to be concluded by it. . . . " (J. Locke, *Two Treatises of Government,* ed. P. Laslett [Cambridge: Cambridge University Press, 1963], p. 350; see chapters 7 and 8 of the *Second Treatise,* esp. pp. 347–51.) However, Locke limited the political obligation of the subject to the case of a constitutionally legitimate government which was acting justly or lawfully towards the "property" of its subjects (see pp. 374, 416–20). But since the Lockeian "right of revolution," as we call it today,

can arise only at the point where these conditions are not fulfilled, the proper exercise of this right effectively annuls any political obligation of any of the subjects to the government. (See here the entire argument of Ch. 19 of the *Second Treatise,* esp. pp. 426, 430, 434, and 437.) It should be noted that the essence of this right, of "rebellion" (as Locke himself called it), is the removal and cancelling of all obligation on the part of the citizens and not the taking up of arms by them. Indeed, the "rebellion" can exist (the return to the "state of war") even though there is no fighting. It also appears, although this is not entirely clear, that Locke lodged the exercise of the right of "rebellion" in the hands of the whole body of "the people," presumably the majority, and not in the hands of the individual citizens severally, as Hobbes had done (see pp. 444–46 but note Locke's odd use of the notion of an "appeal to Heaven").

5. Godwin is what today would be called an *act* utilitarian, of a rather extreme sort. This is particularly evident in his discussion of promise-keeping. (See W. Godwin, *Enquiry Concerning Political Justice,* ed. K. Codell Carter [abridged ed.; Oxford: at the Clarendon Press, 1971], pp. 102–04; for Godwin's act utilitarianism see p. 74 and the editor's introduction, p. xiii.) For Godwin's act utilitarian view of political obligation note the following passages: (a) "The only principle which can be substituted in the room of [statute] law, is that of reason exercising an uncontrolled jurisdiction upon the circumstances of the case" (p. 275; see also pp. 88 and 116); (b) "[I]t is by no means a necessary consequence, that we should disapprove of all the measures of government; but there must be disapprobation, wherever there is a question of strict political obedience" (p. 124). It should, of course, be noted that Godwin's critique of government and of political obligation contained other lines of argument than the one I have briefly discussed here.

6. It is more like Godwin's for another reason as well. It should be noted that Godwin used not only the act-utilitarian argument to which I have been referring but also one where the notion of autonomy was set against that of obedience to law. (See the *Enquiry,* pp. 118–21 and, also, pp. 46 and 286.) In this respect Godwin anticipated Wolff's argument, or at least a variant of it; although his was nowhere near as clear or well worked out as Wolff's. Apparently what Godwin particularly objected to was the claim that obedience to the will of another in law, which rested ultimately on the sanctions of coercive force, should be thought to rest on some sort of reverence or respect. That he did not, however, believe in a complete autonomy of the individual is evident, especially from pages 221–22.

7. Although Wolff's notion of a "genuine incompatibility" is developed as being between *authority* and autonomy, I am, for reasons given in the

text, treating of the incompatibility as being between *obligation* and autonomy. I would also take it that Wolff's talk about the notion of *de jure* authority being a "round square" sort of thing really attaches, then, to the notion of political obligation. (See *Defense of Anarchism,* p. 71 for the phrases quoted, and also pp. 18–19.)

8. Jeffrey Reiman's argument, in his book *In Defense of Political Philosophy* (New York: Harper Torchbooks, 1972), is a good example of the reversal I am discussing: making authority the prior concept rather than obligation. Moreover, he drops the notion of a *strict* obligation to obey the laws (see esp. pp. 42–43). But, nonetheless, his argument remains externally grounded in that he simply identifies justified political authority with *morally* justified political authority (see pp. 44–45 and 53–55).

9. Bernard Gert lists "Obey the law" as one of ten justified moral rules, among which he also numbers such rules as "Don't deceive" and "Keep your promise." (See *The Moral Rules: A New Rational Foundation for Morality* [New York: Harper Torchbooks, edition of 1973; originally published, 1966], p. 125, and, also, pp. 114–18, 120–21, 224–25.)

10. I am thinking here not so much of the case of being under obligation to *a* law as of being in a state of "allegiance"; allegiance is a relation to laws, a relation of principled compliance to lawfulness, by virtue of these laws' being authoritatively issued. For an interesting and balanced treatment here, see M. M. Goldsmith, *Allegiance* (University of Exeter, inaugural lecture of November 1970).

11. I have dealt with some of the issues raised in this paper in more extended discussions elsewhere. On the topic of *civil disobedience,* see "Civil Disobedience," *Ethnics* 80.2 (January 1970), 123–39; and Conscientious Actions and the Concept of Civil Disobedience," in P.A. French (ed.), Conscientious Actions: *The Revelation of the Pentagon Papers* (Cambridge, Mass.: Schenkman/General Learning Press, 1974), pp. 36–52. For an elaboration of the treatment of *punishment,* see "On the Logic of Justifying Legal Punishment," *Am. Philos. Q.* 7.3 (July 1970), 253–59. On the subject of *anarchism,* see "Wolff's Defense of Philosophical Anarchism," *Philosophical Quarterly, 24,* (April 1974), 140–49. A summary of the basic argument of this paper is presented, in somewhat different form, in "Two Models for Justifying Authority," *Ethnics* 86.1 (October 1975).

The Nature and Function of Epistemic Authority

Richard T. De George

DURING the past several years challenges to authority have raised questions about its nature, function, and legitimacy. It is quite clear that many of the justifications for authority which were previously given and which are still sometimes given will simply no longer do. But those who challenge authority are no more clear in their protest than those who attempt to uphold authority are in its defense. Consequently there is need to get clear what authority means and what its possible justifications and limits are. In this paper I shall first outline a framework for dealing with this topic. I shall then analyze in some detail a particular and often neglected type of authority, which I shall call 'epistemic authority.' I shall conclude by applying the results of my analysis to the domain of morality.

I

The word 'authority' is and has been used in a great many ways. As with so many key terms in philosophy, there is no single, univocal meaning which we can fall back on. The concept of authority embraces a rather large variety of types, all of which are more or less related in some way. I shall not claim to do justice to this whole

---

*Portions of this article are based on my article, "The Functions and Limits of Epistemic Authority." *The Southern Journal of Philosophy*, VIII (1970), pp. 199-204.

family of authorities; rather I shall briefly distinguish and characterize a number of the more common types.

We can speak of a person being an authority, as when we say "He
is an authority on Hegel," or "He is an authority in New Testament
scholarship"; we can speak of a person having authority, as "He has
the authority to perform marriages," or when we say "He is an authorized representative"; we can speak of people exercising authority; and we can speak of things embodying authority, as when we
speak of "the authority of the law," or when we refer to a set of
rules being "the final authority in a game." People can also speak
with authority, whether or not they are authorities.

Now it is not my intention to choose any one of these uses as
primary, and it is my contention that no one use is basic or has
privileged status. Yet I think we can discover a certain formal structure which most uses exemplify, and which is a necessary though not
a sufficient component of the concept of authority. In all cases authorty is either a relation or a relational quality attributable to a
person or office or document or set of rules. In all cases we have a
bearer of authority related to those persons (or functions or things)
for whom (or over which) he is the authority. To be an authority or
to have authority without there being a subject or subjects to whom,
for whom, or over whom one is or has authority would make no
sense. But authority is not simply a diadic relation between the
bearer and the subject. It is impossible to be an authority in general;
authority is always and necessarily related to some field or area of
competence or applicability over which the authority is exercised.
All authority is thus essentially a relation among a *bearer*, a *subject*,
and a *field,* in virtue of a particular quality, attribute, or context. This
latter component supplies the justification for the legitimate use of
authority, and it varies from type to type. There is no one thing or
quality which makes authority legitimate, and to search for any such
component is to search in vain. The core relation of authority can
be put formally by saying that "A is an authority for B over field C
in virtue of D" (or in some contexts authority is the right or power
of A to do B with respect to some field C in virtue of D).

To have said this is not to have said very much. It leaves open
all questions about the content of authority and the different kinds

of authority. But it does suggest ways of ascertaining, specifying, and so perhaps delimiting the extent of authority. The relation between bearer and subject will lead us to investigate other factors about each, and the field and justification will yield principles of limitation to the exercise of authority.

We can divide authority into two broad classifications which we can call 'epistemic authority' (declarative-emotive) and 'deontic' (performatory) authority. The first corresponds roughly to what R. S. Peters refers to as someone's being "an authority"; the second to what he refers to as someone being "in authority."

We might then speak of authority based on knowledge, in virtue of which one person can be an authority for another in a given field in which he holds superiority over that other; the authority of a saint in matters of morality or holiness, accruing to him because of his virtue, the authority of an artist because of the execution of his art in a distinctive way. Each of these follows the pattern of what I shall call 'epistemic authority,' and, though it would be tempting to call this authority 'personal' since it is vested in a person because of his specific qualities, this should not be taken to mean that there is no objective basis and justification of which it is susceptible.

In the realm of deontic or performatory authority we can distinguish imperial authority, exercised by a state through its government and its various organs; paternalistic authority, exercised by a parent over his minor children, and by extension the authority of anyone standing in *loco parentis* over either minors or over those who are in some way not considered to be completely competent to care for themselves; and operative authority, which is vested in any designated leader or office by a group, freely formed for the purpose of achieving some common end.

The list is not exhaustive, nor are the types necessarily mutually exclusive. The same person may exercise paternalistic authority over his children in virtue of his position and their need, he may have authority over them which is sanctioned by law, he may be their moral model, and he may be respected by them as an epistemic authority in numerous areas of knowledge. A leader of a state may have duly constituted imperial authority and exercise epistemic authority as well in a certain field.

In each case the justification for the authority varies, as do the kind and extent of authority. Each type may also be either *de facto* or *de jure*, legitimate or illegitimate; effective or ineffective; and formal or informal. To understand each type with any fullness it should be seen in its relation to the concepts associated with it and distinguished from it, such as responsibility, obedience, freedom, law, force, coercion, respect, and so on. Finally, in seeking the justification for authority, we can distinguish a justification for authority in general or for particular kinds in general, from particular institutionalizations of authority or from particular instances of the use of authority within that institution. An anarchist might deny that any imperial authority is legitimate; a democrat may deny the legitimacy of a totalitarian type of imperial authority, but acknowledge the legitimacy of a certain democratic type of authority; and within such a system one might hold that a given official, e.g., the President, though he has legitimate authority in certain realms, exceeded that authority in performing a certain act or giving a certain order. The various levels of justification should be kept distinct, though they are too often confused.

II

With this very rough sketch, let me now turn to a closer analysis of one type of authority, epistemic authority.

Deontic or performative authority involves or yields power, whether it be the power to command another or to act for him. Epistemic authority, I shall argue, does not. In this sense it is impotent. Power may be thrust upon the bearers of such authority, but it cannot legitimately be demanded by them simply because of their epistemic authority. By dealing with this type of authority I hope to underline in passing the fact that not all authority follows the paradigm of political authority.

As we have noted, epistemic authority is authority which is based on knowledge. It is in virtue of his knowledge, for instance, that we say, "Professor Knowitall is an authority on Hegel," or "Dr. Skillful is an authority on heart surgery." Epistemic authority is relational because part of the function of claiming that *x* is an authority is that others with less knowledge would do well to listen to him if they want to learn about the field in which he is knowledgeable. An un-recognized savant may be a legitimate epistemic authority; but if he is not recognized, either formally or informally, he is not a *de facto* authority at all.

As a formal definition of *de facto* epistemic authority I propose the following: *x* (the bearer of authority) is an epistemic authority for *y* (the subject of authority), if, because of his belief in *x*'s superior knowledge, *y* holds some proposition *p*, which *x* has enunciated (or which *y* believes *x* has enunciated), to be true or more probably true than he did before *x* enunciated it.[1]

This scheme is open to a great variety of substitutions. X need not be a person, and for *x* we might substitute a text or other written work or document; or *x* might be the fund of knowledge of a discipline accepted by *y*, a practioner within that discipline. The scheme does not preclude any specific instance of authority based on knowledge. It does however link epistemic authority to the acknowledgment of that authority by the subject of authority. Thus, no matter how authoritatively *x* may speak, or how legitimate an authority he may be, he does not have *de facto* authority unless his utterances are believed. Conversely, *x* may be a *de facto* epistemic authority for *y*, though in fact *x* is not a legitimate authority, and there are no good reasons for *y* to believe what *x* asserts. Though the scheme characterizes *de facto* epistemic authority, my analysis will also raise the question of legitimacy, i.e., the question of when *y* might *reasonably* accept *x* as an epistemic authority.

Several things follow simply from the definition. If *x* and *y* had equal knowledge, there would be no reason for either *x* or *y*—both of whom know *p* to be true on independent grounds—to hold *p* to be more certain simply because the other had enunciated it. The statement of one chemistry professor to another that water is composed of two parts hydrogen and one part oxygen, for instance, should not make the latter more certain of the truth of the statement than he was before. The same statement made by the chemistry professor to his students might well make them more certain of its truth than before he uttered it; in which case he would be an epistemic authority for them.

Secondly, one can in some cases be an authority for himself. It makes no sense in the present tense, for me to believe any proposition to be true simply because I utter it. But knowing myself, the fact that I had said something previously might be good reason for my believing it to be the case now, though I have forgotten the reasoning, proof, or grounds for my uttering it then.

Thirdly, to be an authority one must usually have organized, systematic knowledge. Someone who has lived through a series of events may be called a witness to them. But he is not automatically an authority on them. Though one has privileged access to one's own thought and feelings, it is not usual to call each of us an authority on himself or his feelings. Yet if someone should so use the term, nothing seems to turn on it. It is subsumable under my proposed definition, which, I repeat, claims to be descriptive and *de facto,* not prescriptive or *de jure;* such authority would be clearly informal, though the line between formal and informal epistemic authority is not always clearcut.

Involved in the very notion of authority is y's holding p to be true or more probably true than before x enunciated it. Consequently epistemic authority clearly implies the possibility of attaining knowledge, though no distinction need be made among rational knowledge, knowledge of fact, knowledge of how to do things, and knowledge or purported knowledge on questions of value. Moreover, if y's belief has any basis and is not simply blind acceptance of what x asserts, epistemic authority involves the double claim that knowledge is attainable and that there is some independent criterion for testing the truth claims of another. One might, though it is not common usage, speak of the authority of reason or of facts, meaning thereby that in some sense men must submit to or conform to reality, or to facts, or to the rules of logic, or to the power of reason, and so on, in order to achieve knowledge. Such submission seems to be quite different from the acceptance of something on the word of another. If one chooses to describe such cases as instances of authority we might refer to such conformity as submission to "logical" or "ontological" authority. The important point is that p is not true simply *because* x says p. As we shall see in more detail shortly, epistemic authority implies the implicit acknowledgment of the possibility of attaining truth independently of x's assertion of p, and the acceptance of certain truth-making criteria or conditions.

Epistemic authority is thus in principle substitutional in nature. Its purpose is to substitute the knowledge of one person in a certain field for the lack of knowledge of another. It is in principle expendable and is always open to challenge. Theoretically, the knowledge of an individual, of a lawyer or of a doctor, of a scholar or of a scientist could, in principle, be acquired by another, thus making the substitution unnecessary.

It is only because others can in fact acquire the knowledge of the bearer of epistemic authority that an epistemic authority can achieve the authority he has. In order for x to be recognized as a legitimate authority in z, it must be possible for others to have sufficient knowledge in that field to be able to test his claims to knowledge. If someone claimed knowledge in a field in which no one else had any knowledge, he could not legitimately be recognized as an authority in that field since no one would be able to establish him as such. Their relation to him and to that field would be based simply on his untested claims, towards which, if my analysis is correct, a certain scepticism would be the more appropriate response. The result is that for x to a legitimate authority for y, y must already know enough about z to know that x knows more about it then he does.[2] If y knows nothing about z, the only other reasonable ground for acknowledging x as an authority is that he has been acknowledged as an authority by someone else or by others whom y believes is (or are) trustworthy and knowledgeable in z so that they can testify to x's knowledge. In this case however y simply takes it on the authority of someone else that he (y) should accept x as an authority; and the acceptance of the word of this someone else requires justification, just as accepting x's word does. Ultimately, (1) y must have *some* knowledge upon which to build if his acknowledgment of x as an epistemic authority is to be anything but blind acceptance; and (2) y must ultimately (and usually implicitly) make an act of faith or trust in whomever he accepts as an epistemic authority.

Any attempt to justify epistemic authority in general should take into account the obvious fact that men are unequal in ability, some being more capable intellectually than others; the fact that some men know more than others; the fact that some data are available only to certain persons appropriately located in space and time; and the fact that there is so much which can be known that no one can know it all. Some men know more than others about certain topics as a result of their individual study, research, thought, experience, or experimentation. For the subject of authority, the bearer of authority serves either as a guide or as a source. By turning to the authority for information, guidance, or advice, he takes advantage of the bearer's superior knowledge. To the layman, a trained lawyer is an epistemic authority on legal matters; for the practicing attorney, a legal scholar or judge may be an authority. For the patient, the doctor is the authority in matters of sicknesses and their cure. For the student, the teacher is or can be an epistemic authority in a certain branch of knowledge. Reliance on authority is a way in which knowledge can be transmitted and shared, so that more men may know and use this knowledge than would otherwise be the case. This, in brief, is the basis for the argument that epistemic authority is in general legitimate. The argument is a pragmatic one, and it claims that in some cases it is reasonable and rational to accept the word of someone else that p is the case.

Society has furthermore found it useful to acknowledge certain classes of authorities, and to accept the formal certification of individuals by the leaders of those classes or their professional organizations. The ground for trusting or believing their certification is again pragmatic, based on how the class or organization demonstrates its knowledge, e.g., in curing the sick, imparting knowledge to engineers that enables them to build houses and bridges which withstand the elements, and so on.

A epistemic authority—a doctor, a lawyer, a teacher—is thus often designated as an authority by those who have some knowledge of the field and who acknowledge that the bearer of authority has knowledge which they verify and in virtue of which they certify him. An epistemic authority can thus initially be named as an authority by others with knowledge; in society this is often formalized, though it need not be. Doctors and lawyers are certified as authorities by medical schools, law schools, or by state examinations, made up and graded by those considered competent in medicine and law. Similarly in the sciences and humanities, a scientist or scholar does work which can and which should be checked by others having the competence to do so before he is certified as an authority by conferring on him a degree or academic rank. But even so certified, x is usually not an authority for those who certify him, since they must generally have superior knowledge for their certification to be acceptable to others. Certification, then, does not make x a *de facto* authority. It only supplies *prima facie* grounds for others to consider him as a legitimate authority.

Since x is a *de facto* authority only if he is believed by y, it is y who makes him a *de facto* authority. He may believe p when uttered by x because he knows enough about the field to know that x knows a great deal and is trustworthy, an inference from past instances of x uttering p's which y has independently verified; or he may accept p when uttered by x because he trusts other x's who have certified him. He accepts their word because society in general does. And he accepts what society in general does, because it seems to work.

Furthermore, it should be clear that y's acknowledgment of x as an epistemic authority need not be an all or nothing matter. He may hold p to be just slightly more probably true than before x asserted it; he may hold p to be certainly true because x asserted it; or he may adopt any intermediate position.

Now the analysis shows the tenuousness of the justification for epistemic authority. It can be challenged at various stages; for the slips between formal certification, the actual possession of knowledge, and the will and ability to transfer it effectively are many; it is always justified inductively; and there is always danger of a misfire and of accepting something as true which is in fact false. Yet it is still reasonable to accept something as true on authority in certain cases.

What limits, then, should subjects of epistemic authority reasonably place on their acceptance of anyone as an epistemic authority?

First, as every schoolboy knows, the epistemic authority granted to a scholar should extend only to the area or field of his demonstrated or certified competence. A noted chemist may wield great authority in chemical circles and on topics concerned with his research; but this does not make him an authority in history or in politics, though the transfer of knowledge in adjacent disciplines and the transfer of scholarly habits of care, toughmindedness, etc., may be worth more than the schoolboy realizes.

Second, we should always remember that epistemic authority is substitutional. Taking something on authority is different from believing it because it has been proven to us or shown to us to be true. For if it has been shown to be true or if it has been proven to us, then we do not need authority as the reason for our belief.

Third, the weight which subjects of epistemic authority initially give to the bearer of this authority should be proportional both to the respect given him or acknowledge him by his peers and to the amount of general agreement there is among those knowledgeable in the field concerning the topic at issue. In an area where there is a consensus about the facts, the statements of a recognized authority are more trustworthy and rightfully carry more weight than in an area in which a man may be competent but in which there is considerable disagreement among the competent. The pronouncement of a certified doctor concerning a fairly common and well recognized ailment is more certain and should be given greater weight than his opinion concerning treatment in a case where there is great dispute. In the latter instance the more noteworthy the doctor the more weight his opinion should carry; but it should be less than in an area where there is consensus among doctors generally.

Fourth, the greater the number of verified statements an authority utters on his topic, the more reasonable it is to accept his other statements as true, other things being equal. It takes many correct and otherwise corroborated statements to justify y's continued acknowledgment of x as an authority; it takes very few cases of detected error to render his epistemic authority dubious.

I indicated earlier that a teacher might be certified as an epistemic authority by his peers and that such certification seems to be sufficient ground for a student to initially acknowledge him as an authority in his field. Let me emphasize the word 'initially,' however. For if my analysis is correct no one can legitimately force any y to acknowledge any x as an epistemic authority. Neither one's peers nor faculty rank can force such an acknowledgment nor can any x legitimately *de-*

mand that any *y* so acknowledge him. A teacher has epistemic authority in a classroom only to the extent that the subjects of that authority, namely his students, grant it to him by acknowledging him as an authority for them. They may be predisposed to doing so, but the teacher should win their acknowledgment from them by his superior knowledge.

Children do well initially to believe what adults tell them because children know so little that they cannot help but learn a great deal that is true and useful from adults, even if they assimilate some falsehoods in the process. Gradually they learn that not all adults are trustworthy and that not everything they are told is true. Most children as they increase in age and experience become more discriminating. Part of their education consists in learning to discriminate among authorities and among the utterances of their teachers, distinguishing fact from hypothesis, reasons from rhetoric, and learning to find things out for themselves, reasoning to them, and verifying them on one's own. Because epistemic authority is substitutional, in university teaching such authority ought not be used by a teacher to replace explanation, demonstration, or argument. For to fall back on authoritative statements is to preclude the education of the students. The aim of the university professor should be not only to serve as a source of information, but to help his students learn how to do what he does, how to check up on what he and others say, how to uncover and evaluate information for themselves. Ultimately a university teacher's goal should be to help his students no longer need him as an authority and to help at least some of them become his peers.

Since epistemic authority cannot be forced, it is inappropriate to expect suspension of judgment with respect to what an authority says in his field. As the student learns more in a field, he should be alert to the limits of his teacher's knowledge. Since the knowledge he receives from *x* is always substitutional, moreover, he should be reluctant to believe *x*'s assertions if they go against something else which he knows either on good authority or from direct evidence or demonstration. In the first instance he faces a clash of authorities and must sort out independent evidence as best he can. In the second instance he has good reason for not believing what he has been told, since arguments from authority in the field of science and scholarship are among the weakest kind.

Finally, epistemic authority carries with it no right to command. Knowledge by itself gives no one the *right* to teach, to act for another, or to impose his views on them. Epistemic authority, which requires initial assent on the part of the subject, involves simply belief, and not any commitment to obedience. It may well be the part of wisdom and of prudence to utilize the knowledge of the learned in relevant ways. Yet, the philosopher has no *right* to be king; an authority in city planning has no right, simply because of his knowledge, to impose his views on any city; a scholar, simply in virtue of his knowledge, has no right to decide how a university class is to be run. Because of his knowledge he may be given operative or organizational authority to make decisions, issue grades, or what have you. But his epistemic and operative authority are distinguishable and should, for clarity's sake, be kept distinct.

I am not saying that a teacher has no authority to make assignments or establish requirements; rather I am saying that he does not have the right to do this in virtue of his *epistemic* authority, but in virtue of some other kind of authority—operative, or legal, or charismatic. For what could the demand or command that others recognize one as an epistemic authority mean? If it means 1) "you have to listen to what I say and know what I say so you can give it back on a test," it is clearly a function of operative authority; if it is 2) equivalent to the claim that "it is reasonable to believe what I say because I know what I am talking about, and it is true, and it will save you much pain and effort," then it is simply another assertion to be believed or not; or if it is 3) a claim that "I know best what you must know and because of this you must do as I say, and I say 'believe this'," then it becomes a type of paternalistic authority. Thus, *x* has no right to demand that *y* believe what he says. And though *y* may act on the basis of what *x* asserts, *x* has no *right* to demand this.

For such reasons it seems to me simply wrong to define epistemic authority as involving the *right* to speak or to be believed, as R. S. Peters and others maintain. A general doctrine of rights may include in it the right of freedom of speech and of the press. But epistemic authority itself involves no rights as ingredient in it. To smuggle them in is to conflate epistemic and other types of authority. Simply because one knows something (or a great deal), whether or not he is acknowledged as an authority, he has no *right* to be heard or to be listened to. Not to listen to someone who has appropriate knowledge may be foolish or imprudent. But no one has the right either to be heard or to be believed simply because of his real or purported knowledge.

Now it might well be objected that truth should have more rights than falsehood, that men have a right to hear the truth, that those who possess it have the obligation to make it known, and so they have the *right* to make it known. Though I am willing to concede all this, it is fully compatible with my claim that epistemic authority carries with it no special right to be heard or to be believed and no right to command. In the first place, a society which wishes to protect truth can do so by guaranteeing the free speech of all, and need make no special rules for epistemic authorities. Its citizenry or leaders may reasonably pay more attention to the utterances of the learned than of others in a great many matters. But the point is that freedom of speech or the right to be heard is a natural or a civil right, and is not a function of knowledge. Secondly, though truth or reason or logic is coercive for the rational man, it is the *demonstration* of truth that is rationally coercive. And when a truth is thus coercively demonstrated, there is no need for authority. Thirdly, the history of human thought has amply shown that the authoritative imposition of belief has often precluded or hindered the development or discovery of other truths. The dangers which result from a state or government claiming it has the truth and imposing it are too well known to need recounting here. Consequently, since the acceptance of p on the basis of authority is often reasonable, this fact and not any supposed right of x is the only legitimate or rationally defensible basis for y acknowledging x as an epistemic authority.

III

We can apply these principles to various areas, and so test their generality and fruitfulness. To illustrate this, I shall turn briefly to the field of ethics. We should keep separate the question of authority in morality, from the question of the possible moral foundation of established authority, and from the question of moral authority as such.

I shall be concerned only with the first of these. The usual approach to a discussion of authority in morals is to dismiss it on the one hand because acceptance of authority would violate the autonomy of the moral agent and on the other because no one is empowered to legislate what is moral and what is not. A moral agent, this view goes, must come to his own decisions if his action is to have moral worth. He must act on imperatives or principles of his own choosing; his conscience or reason must be his guide. Furthermore, an authority could issue commands or prohibitions either arbitrarily or for good reasons. If he did so arbitrarily, there is no need to heed him; if he has good reasons, then the reasons can be discovered independently by the right use of reason, and there is no need for the authority.

This view, however, fails to consider either authority or morality closely enough.

The proper model for authority in morals is not that of someone in authority issuing commands which must be followed. If this were the case, we could properly reject the moral lawgiver; for it is always possible to ask whether what he commands is moral. Rather the proper analogy is to be found in epistemic authority.

Consider, first of all, that—whether moral judgments are cognitive, emotive, or a mixture of both—morality is taught, together with language, science, etc. Parents teach their children that certain acts are wrong or considered wrong either by the parents or by society or by both. There are certain minimal moral rules which seem necessary for any society, and a great many other rules peculiar to each. But morality is taught to the young and taken by them, at least initially, as knowledge of proper behavior .

The general principles we discerned with respect to epistemic autority seem clearly to be appropriate here. A child naturally accepts what he is taught in morals, as in other spheres, until he finds that it is contradicted by his experience or until he finds that other persons who are equally qualified as his parents hold different views. In an extremely homogeneous society he may find great unanimity on the part of all the adults he encounters and this unanimity increases the rationality of his believing what he is taught concerning morals.

Where the stated principles are violated in action, or where adults disagree as to what is right and wrong, the authority of each is diminished and the epistemic moral authority of all is properly questionable.

The moral rules taught children, those publicly and commonly upheld and preached in a society, can be called conventional morality. If the morality is that of a peer group in a society with differing moralites, it might be called conformity morality. Such a morality is made up of certain rules or principles, it may be held up as an ideal, and it may be practiced to a greater or less extent from habit and in response to pressures from family, peers, or public opinion. But this is not what most moral philosophers are concerned with. Their concern is with autonomous morality, a personally appropriated morality; a morality willingly and conscientiously adhered to by an individual and upon reflection, for valid reasons. Such a morality, of course, does not spring full grown from the head of Zeus or of anyone else. It is the result not only of individual effort but of individual effort on what is supplied by conventional morality, by society, by saints and sages and philosophers, by one's parents and teachers and friends. And it is only the rare individual who is capable of reaching his own synthesis after mature reflection.

However, the moral man is not simply the one who knows what is right, but who acts on it (some Kantians would add that he acts *because* he knows it is the right way to act).

We can distinguish the philosopher or moral theologian who has knowledge of what is right or good and who in his own action is no better and perhaps worse than other men, from the saint who acts heroically on the basis of what he believes to be the proper way to act.

Now if we remember that in order to grant anyone epistemic authority y must know something about the field and enough to know that x knows more than y does, we can see where and when it would be reasonable to acknowledge an authority in morality. The moral agent should understand what it means to be moral and to think in moral terms. If he does not, he may simply do as he is told or advised from habit or fear or inclination or laziness. But if he does know what it means to be moral and if he wishes to be moral, he may well seek moral guidance, and, I would argue, properly so. In full knowledge of the diversity of moral opinion and the dubiousness of finding the complete truth, he may judge on the basis of his own experience who it is who can guide him in moral matters, either because that person seems to know more or seems to act better than he himself. He may seek the knowledge, clear thinking, and the approach to problems in the light of principle which is supplied by the scholar; or he may seek the insight of someone who appears to him to be holy or at least morally commendable; or he may emulate the example of some saint or moral hero.

To so act is to act morally in the attempt to correct or form one's conscience. The autonomy of conscience does not mean that it is *sui generis* and cut off from the moral experience and knowledge of others. Conscience should not be forced or coerced, but its autonomy is consistent with information and guidance, held on faith from others. Ultimately it means that one must himself decide to act, if the action is a moral act, by the best means he can. One must decide whether to take advice, act on guidance, or adhere to values embodied by others; and then accept the moral risk and responsibility of so acting.

The phrase "the authority of one's conscience" is a vague and possibly misleading one. If our analysis of epistemic authority is correct, one cannot be a present authority for himself. My uttering a proposition is no more a reason for my believing it to be true then my uttering it ten times in succession would be for me to be ten times surer of it than I was before. One's conscience is not independent of him. It is his practical reason (or his practical reason with his attitudes and feelings) relative to certain considered actions. To speak of the authority of conscience is the same as saying that eventually one must decide for himself how to act.

I have been dealing with authority in morality and I have been claiming that it has a legitimate place, just as it does in the sphere of knowledge in general. But just as knowledge in other areas gives no one the right to act for or on others simply because of that knowledge, similarly with epistemic moral authority. One so recognized has no right to command or force others to act in accordance with his beliefs or judgments. The holy man may well inspire others to act as he does; he may preach that they should so act; but he has no right to force them to so act. The reason for this is twofold. The first is that no knowledge carries with it the right to command; the second is that to coerce an action is to rob it of one of the factors usually considered necessary for it to carry moral worth for the doer, viz., that he freely choose the action.

The latter caveat, however, should not be taken as a solution to the controversy over whether morality shold be legislated. The only point I am making here is that one's knowledge or purported knowledge of what is moral is not sufficient justification for imposing it on others either by command or by law. Parents may demand their children act in cerain ways, and societies may demand that their citizens act in certain ways; they have no moral right to command what is immoral; but their right to command or legislate what they think is moral cannot stem simply from their claimed knowledge, and must be conjoined with something more. The 'more' are the institutional facts that make sense out of and justify deontic authority or the authority to command, and these must in their turn be examined and justified.

One who knows that his country should not engage in a war or who knows that his fellow citizens should not discriminate against anyone on the basis of color does not thereby have the right to peremptorily dicate their actions. He may have the obligation to do what he can to change the laws of his country or the attitudes of his fellow citizens. His obligation stems from his moral beliefs. But just as in other realms an epistemic authority cannot legitimately impose his belief on others, so in the moral realm he cannot legitimately impose his belief or demand the action which appropriately follows on that belief simply on the basis of his purported or actual moral knowledge. A just society should be responsive to moral claims, just as it should be to truth claims. But its proper use of deontic authority can and should be distinguished from the proper limits of the epistemic authority of itself or of any of its members.

I started by mentioning the challenges to authority which have been taking place during the past several years. The opposition to parental, operative, and imperial authority is well known. There has also been a breakdown in the acceptance of epistemic authority which in many cases is both understandable and justified. Where the basis for granting epistemic authority in a classroom situation is lacking, student dissatisfaction is both understandable and justifiable; if it is demanded instead of earned, it is rarely given. Where knowledge is the claimed basis for action, epistemic authority need not be invoked. Yet it is sometimes appealed to when knowledge is in fact absent or not available. The rising number of 'credibility gaps' in various areas of social and public life is a reasonable consequence. Even where there is no question of withholding information, the fragmentation and specialization of knowledge make each of us unable to check on many supposed knowledge claims and make us unable to know when reasonably to accept the knowledge claims of another and so when to acknowledge another as an epistemic authority. The enormous growth of knowledge also makes suspect anyone's ability to know all he should to make decisions of worldwide importance. Scepticism and a loss of confidence in the ability of anyone to govern wisely is an understandable if unhappy result.

Epistemic authority is only one of several types of authority, and our analysis has and can take us only so far. Current unrest undoubtedly stems in part from abuses and from failure to clarify the uses and limits of the various kinds of authority to which people are subject. Analysis can be fruitfully used to clarify some of the issues in the current revolt against authority, and to help replace violence with reason. This paper has been an attempt to clear a small part of the tangled thicket. It is obvious that much remains to be done.

NOTES

1. Cf. J. M. Bochenski, "On Authority," *Memorias del XIII Congreso Internacional de Filosofía,* México, Universidad Nacional Autónoma de México, Vol. V, pp. 45-46. I am indebted to an earlier version of that paper, read at a meeting at Notre Dame in 1961, for this approach to epistemic authority.

2. Even in the case of knowledge of one's private experiences, which seems to be an exception, y justifiably recognizes x as an authority only if y knows from his own case the nature of private experiences in general and either has reason to believe, or no reason to doubt, that x is truthful, a careful observer, etc.

The Function and Limits of Moral Authority

W. H. Werkmeister

THE title of my paper seems to imply as an unquestionable fact that there is such a thing as "moral authority" and that everybody somehow knows what it is. How else could we speak of its function and its limits? Actually, however, our problem begins right here; for our first question must be: What is meant by "moral authority"? And the answer to this question is by no means either simple or clear. The difficulty arises because of the ambiguity of the term "authority" itself.

In its primary sense the term means "legal or rightful power"—the right to legislate, to administer, to enforce. Beyond this it means the "rightful power" to settle disputes by judicial decree—such as the power of the United States Supreme Court. But the term "authority" is also used as, in effect, a synonym for the term "expert"—as one having special knowledge or skill in some particular field. So understood, however, the term "authority" does not imply legally grounded power. It signifies merely a degree of acknowledged superiority in certain respects, in certain fields of human endeavor. But, as Professor De George had shown in his very suggestive discussion of "epistemic authority," the distinctions I have just made do not really clarify what is or what can be meant by "moral authority." To make my point, I shall briefly consider Professor De George's application of his interpretation of "epistemic authority" to morality, and shall then indicate further difficulties that arise in this area.

Professor De George quite rightly states that we must "keep separate the question of authority in morality, from the question of the possible moral foundation of established authority, and from the question of moral authority as such." He tells us that he is "concerned only with the first of these" problems; but the crux of the matter, it seems to me, is the third problem—the problem of "moral authority as such"—and I shall be chiefly concerned with it.

Professor De George's basic theme is that "the proper model of authority in morals . . . is to be found in epistemic authority." It will therefore be necessary to examine briefly what is meant by "epistemic authority."

"Any attempt to justify epistemic authority in general," we are told ,"should take into account the obvious fact that . . . some men know more than others about certain topics as a result of their individual study, research, thought, experience, or experimentation." That is to say, we should take into account that some men are "experts" in certain fields. And it must be granted at once that "epistemic authority" so understood "carries with it no special right to be heard or to be believed and no right to command." The vindication of its "authority" lies in the fact that the knowledge involved is subject to objective (i.e., to rational and/or empirical) criteria and is therefore independently testable. When the assumed special knowledge or skill of the "expert" fails to meet these criteria, he no longer has any standing as an "authority" in his field.

Obviously, however, there are variations and degrees in "epistemic authority"; and these, it seems to me, are relevant to our problem. There are, for example, the "innovators" in science—the Newtons, the Einsteins, the Diracs—whose achievements mark the great turning-points in the history of science. "Experts" they are; there can be no questions about that. However, it is their work rather than their "authority" that has carried the day.

But there are other "experts"—in anthropology, for example—who, living for years in a primitive society, learn through intimate and daily contact what life in that society was like before contact with civilization destroyed it, and who thus become an "authority" on the language, the customs, the institutions, the dominant world-view of that society. Under the conditions stated, their experience can never be repeated; but they remain "authorities" in their field.

There are, of course, numerous degrees and variations of "epistemic authority" between these two extremes; and this fact is important when we turn to the problem of "authority in morals."

Professor De George begins by pointing out that "morality is taught," and that for the child his parent, who teaches him that "certain minimal moral rules" should be observed, is an "authority in morals." This is true, of course, for the child who simply trusts his parents. Sooner or later, however, problems arise that entail a challenge to the parent's "authority." Can the philosopher or the theologian ever occupy a place of "authority in morals" comparable to that of the parent? Surely, the philosopher at least should never try to do so—even if he could; for philosophy is not indoctrination.

Granted that "pressures from family, peers, or public opinion" may tend to force the child to live by the "rules" which his parent (or somebody else) has taught him. But this is no longer a matter of force, no matter how indirectly or how subtly that force is applied. And, as Professor De George says so well: "One's knowledge or purported knowledge of what is moral is no sufficient justification for imposing it on others either by command or by law."

But if this is so, then in what sense is the conception of "epistemic authority"—no matter how valuable it may be in itself—the proper model for "authority in morals"? It cannot be such a model when taken in the sense of the "authority" of the great innovators in science; for there is not even a universal agreement as to what the criteria of an objectively valid theory of morals ought to be. Nor can "epistemic authority" be a model in the sense of the anthropologist's "authoritative" knowledge of a particular tribal society; for knowledge of this type is descriptive rather than normative. It informs us as to what is being done in a given society (perchance even in our own), not what ought to be done. But if "epistemological authority" is thus hardly a "proper model" for "authority in morals" —although it may well be a model for theoretical ethics and for the history of morals—it is even less a model for "moral authority."

I fully agree with Professor De George that "analysis can be fruitfully used to clarify some of the issues in the current revolt against authority, and to help replace violence with reason." I would merely add that such analysis cannot rest upon an appeal to "authority"— moral or otherwise. And the "current revolt against authority" is a revolt largely against the institutionalized legislative, administrative, and enforcement authority that is tradition-bound, and against prevailing discriminatory mores in an affluent post-industrial society. Participants in these revolts have more often than not seen their activities primarily as moral responses to specific issues—responses engendered by what was regarded as an intolerable discrepancy between the professed idealism of our socio-economic and political philosophy, on the one hand, and the harsh realities of our society in action, on the other. In the perspective of such conflicts the problem of "moral authority"—of its function and its limits—arises with particular urgency.

Let us now reconsider the problem without further reference to "epistemic authority," for at issue is not cognition in the realm of morals but the authority of A to prescribe a particular course of action for B.

A has such authority over B if, and only if, B accepts A's command as sufficient reason for doing X, and therefore demands no further explanation. But the special status of A in this relationship may be the result of two quite different sets of conditions. Under the first set, A is established on a *de jure* basis as institutionalized moral authority. As God's vicar on earth, the Head of the Roman Catholic Church may thus in some respects be seen as "moral authority" in this sense. Under the second set of conditions, the "moral authority" of A is rooted in what Max Weber has called the charismatic character of A. In this sense the moral innovator, the "prophet," is an "authority": "It is written . . . But I say unto you."

But our problem does not end here; for the facts are that both types of "moral authority"—the *de jure* and the charismatic—have been and can be challenged. Whatever authority they have is acceptable only to their willing followers. But if their authority is to be challenged successfully, this can be done only through reference to an "authority" that is recognized as unchallengeable; and I submit that this "authority" for the ultimate appeal must be principles rather than persons—principles upon which the validity of moral judgments depends. In this respect, I agree, the problem of "moral authority" is comparable to what we encounter as ultimate "authority" in our most advanced sciences—principles rather than persons. But whereas the propositions and laws of science are descriptive and therefore verifiable, moral judgments serve a normative function. They do not tell us what is the case, but what ought to be done—and thus are not verifiable in any epistemic sense.

The emotivists have made the most of this fact in their *one-sided way*.[1] Although it is true that moral judgments are usually, if not always, accompanied by feelings and attitudes of the speaker, they are not simply expressions of those feelings or attitudes. Nor do the feelings and attitudes invest the judgments with moral significance. On the contrary, it is the judgments that render the feelings objectively significant, and that intrinsically justify acts of approval or disapproval. And it is the judgments, not the feelings or attitudes, that can be objectively validated, and that therefore provide a basis for "moral authority."

What is important to note here is that moral judgments, being prescriptive rather than descriptive, cannot be verified in any epistemic sense but can be validated by being subsumed under broad principles of conduct that are generally accepted as binding.

Such principles, however, are themselves acceptable only when the actions and the goals of actions which they enjoin serve permanent human interests and, ultimately, the interests of all mankind. That is to say, the principles themselves are acceptable if, and only if, they define an ideal of individual and social existence that satisfies most profoundly the requirements of being human. An appeal to such an ideal is at once an appeal to reason and to inescapable facts of experience which involve our deepest affective needs and integrative responses. Moral judgments rooted in such an ideal have a normative persuasiveness expressive of the ideal itself, and therefore have the "authority" of the ideal. There is and can be no other "moral authority."

That in the conception of the ideal various cognitive factors are involved is, of course, obvious. The ideal itself, however, is not cognitive. It is the projection of a value-pattern as norm for human existence, and it has the "authority" of a norm. If this is so, then a moral judgment—i.e., the approval or disapproval of some specific mode of behavior—is never merely an expression of feeling or of a personal, emotion-charged attitude. It derives its "authority" from the fact that it contributes to the realization of the ideal in the lives of men. If it does not function in this way, it loses its "authority" and can be brushed aside readily on purely personal grounds.

So long as the normative value-pattern incorporated in the ideal is generally accepted by the members of a social group, its "authority" serves as a fulcrum for the "moral" evaluation of all institutions, customs, and laws that exist within that group or are proposed for it. That is to say, the "moral authority" of the normative ideal as manifested in appropriate evaluative judgments thus functions as a selective agent in the dynamic of social evolution, and as a guide to constructive actions that may transform the whole existing pattern of a given society. There is much of this sort of transvaluation discernible in the widespread unrest of our times. Civil rights legislation, for example, is but a belated effort to bring the actualities of our society into at least a semblance of harmony with the moral ideal expressed in the Declaration of Human Rights to which we stand committed. It is the "authority" of the ideal that morally justifies the agitation and the pressures for social reform.

When the moral judgment is no longer seen as representative of the normative ideal, it loses its objective validity and, with it, its moral character as well. It is then merely an expression of personal predilections and should be treated as such.

But the normative ideal itself may be challenged—not only in details but in its entirety. What Nietzsche called "the spirit of nihilism" may force upon us a complete transvaluation of values. Or a "new prophet"—a Lenin, a Mao-Tse-tung—may challenge the old order: "But I say unto you." Whenever this happens, we face the question of what does it mean to exist as a human being? What, in an ultimate sense, will truly satisfy our essential needs, our profoundest aspirations as human beings?

It is in answer to these questions that we must evaluate any proposal for a normative ideal and, in the end, must project as our own that value-pattern which most adequately serves as an ideal of human existence. It must be noted, however, that this ultimate decision is existentialist-ontological rather than moral. There is no "moral authority" that rightfully determines the outcome, for "moral authority" itself depends upon it—i.e., it depends upon the ontologically justifiable normative ideal.

And let it be noted that the projection of the ideal is cognitively justifiable. The ideal itself, however, is normative rather than cognitive. And it is in its normative character that it functions as "moral authority" or as the basis for such "authority."

Despite all its limitations and its lack of absoluteness, "moral authorty" is thus ontologically grounded; and from this fact derives its character as "authority"—not from the status (*de jure* or charismatic) of some particular person or personal agency. "Moral authority" is what it is—in its very nature and function, and with all its limitations—because it is entailed by the basic, the most profound requirements of human existence as human; because, that is, man can and does exist as truly human only when he exists as a moral being.

NOTES

1. For a detailed criticism of their position see my *Theories of Ethics: A Study in Moral Obligation*, Johnsen Publishing Company, Lincoln, Nebraska, 1961, pp. 17-87.

The Functions and Limits of Political Authority

Michael D. Bayles

IN his paper "The Nature and Function of Epistemic Authority," Richard De George notes that both defenders and critics of authority have been unclear about what they are defending or criticizing.[1] There is some reason for different views of what authority is. The functions and limits of authority, at least political authority, do vary with the justification offered. The different functions and limits ascribed to political authority by traditional political philosophers such as Hobbes, Locke, and Rousseau derived from differences in the justification they offered for it. Nevertheless, clarification of the formal structure of the concept of political authority must precede any justification of its uses and limits.

THE CONCEPT OF POLITICAL AUTHORITY

Authority may be roughly divided into that over belief and that over conduct. For example, the authority of an expert on Etruscan art primarily pertains to beliefs while that of a policemen pertains to conduct. Of course this distinction is only one of emphasis, for belief and conduct are interdependent. Hence, there are mixed cases such as the authority of an engineer on how to build bridges. Nevertheless, most people view political authority as concerned with what they do, not what they believe.

Since both authority and power over another person pertain to his conduct, the relation between these two concepts has been the subject of much discussion. Some philosophers have held that authority is a form of power while others have held that authority and power are distinct and mutually exclusive concepts. Much of this debate may perhaps be avoided by distinguishing between an ordinary and a social scientific concept of one person having power over another.

For purposes of social science, it is useful to have a term designating all the ways in which one person may affect the behavior of another. Yet no ordinary English term appears to have such a use. Thus, 'power' has frequently been used for this concept. With this concept a person, X, has power over another, Y, with respect to actions of type A if (1) X is able to perform an action of type B, and (2) if X does so act, Y is more disposed to perform an action of type. A.[2] This concept can have a broad or narrow sense depending upon whether or not it is also required that X intend or desire that Y do A. For present purposes only the narrower sense in which X intends that Y do A is relevant.

The relations between X and Y designated by this social scientific concept of power may be of two kinds. In one kind, X's ability to affect Y's conduct depends upon his intending to do something for, or to, Y if Y does or does not do A. X intends to reward or harm Y if Y does or does not do A. For example, if X bribes Y he intends to confer a benefit upon Y for doing A. In the other kind of social scientific power X does not intend to reward or harm Y for doing A. For example, if X persuades Y that it would be best to do A, he does not intend to reward or harm Y.

To clearly mark the difference between the social scientific and ordinary concepts of power, the social scientific concept shall be designated power$_1$ and the ordinary concept power$_2$. The ordinary concept only pertains to the first kind of power$_1$ in which rewards or harms are intended. It is unclear whether the ordinary concept applies to all instances of this kind of power$_1$ or not. It tends to be restricted to cases in which the intended reward or harm is thought to be very important. In any case, the clearest cases of power$_2$ are those in which X coerces Y. Thus, power$_2$ tends to be identified with coercion.

Authority, on the other hand, pertains to the second kind of power$_1$ in which rewards or harms are not intended. If X has authority over Y he need not threaten, harm, or promise rewards to get Y to do A. X can get Y to perform actions by telling, commanding, or ordering him to do them. Thus, power$_2$ and authority appear to be mutually exclusive. But it is only the exercise of them on a specific occasion which is mutually exclusive. That is, if X promises benefits or threatens harms to Y to get him to do something, then he does not exercise authority. But a person may possess or have both authority and power$_2$ over another. That is, X may be able to get Y to do something either by merely telling him to do so or by threatening him. Usually, power$_2$ is not exercised if a person has authority, for the use of authority is more efficient and less "costly."

Since insofar as X has authority over Y he need not intend rewards or harms to get Y to do A, then Y must in some sense accept X's directives as reasons for doing A. It is at this point that the distinction between authority over conduct or belief becomes difficult. For Y may accept X's directives as reasons for doing A because he believes X's judgment about what should be done is more likely to be correct than his own. Thus, a person attempting to disarm a bomb will accept the directives of a demolitions expert. In these cases X's directives are accepted because X is *an authority* on how to do something. On the other hand, Y may accept X's directives because X is *in authority*. Y accepts X's directives because he recognizes X as occupying a position or role entitling him to issue directives.[3]

Most but not all instances of political authority involve X being in a position of authority. The major exception concerns charismatic political rulers such as Napoleon. Of course the two bases for accepting X's directives are mutually reinforcing. It is sometimes said that one should be very cautious in criticizing the President's decisions in foreign affairs because his position provides him with information others do not have, so his judgments are more likely to be correct. On the other hand, it is also said that a person probably would not be in a position of authority unless he had shown good judgment about such matters. Nevertheless, the rest of this paper limits political authority to that involved in a person being in a position of authority and ignores claims that the person's judgment is more likely to be correct than that of others.

Positions of authority are determined by rules. Usually a person must meet certain conditions to occupy a position of authority, e. g., be elected or appointed. Further, he may be required to issue directives in a certain manner, e.g., in writing. The directives may only apply to certain persons, e.g., the members of a union, and cover certain subjects, e.g., union and work affairs but not leisure time activities. Finally, the position has a purpose or goal, e.g., an auditor is to make sure the books are accurate. Hence, the general form of rules constituting positions of authority is as follows: Person X, with qualifications Q, may issue directives D, in manner M, to person(s) Y, concerning subject S, for the purpose P.

Various moral or deontic relations and conditions may arise from such a rule and confusion about them has obscured many discussions of authority. First, one must distinguish between those deontic conditions pertaining to positions of authority and those pertaining to persons entitled to occupy such positions. For example, a rather common definition of such authority as "the right to command, and correlatively, the right to be obeyed" obscures this distinction.[4] If X has met the qualifications for occupying a position of authority, then he has a right to that position. Correlatively, others have a duty to accord him that position. But they do not have a duty to obey his directives. For example, a president of a corporation may have a duty to install a man as vice-president, but he does not have a duty to obey him.

More fundamentally, a position of authority does not involve a right to command or issue directives. Instead, it involves what in legal systems is called (in yet another sense) power$_3$. Power$_3$ indicates the ability specified by rules to issue directives or do other things such as perform marriages. The correlative of power$_3$ is the liability of others to having such things done.[5] It does not involve a *duty* of obedience. Nonetheless, those liable to the exercise of power$_3$ may have an *obligation* to follow directives issued by a person with power$_3$ if the rule creating that position is obligatory upon them. Whether or not it is obligatory upon them depends upon its justifiability. For example, if the members of a club had all promised to follow a rule permitting the executive committee to establish dues, then they would have an obligation to follow a directive of the committee to pay dues of ten dollars each. In short, the obligation to authority is an obligation to conform to a rule constituting a position of authority. Since the obligation is not to a person, it does not entail a correlative right.[6] Consequently, one has an obligation to follow the directives of a person in a position of authority, but only if the directives are in conformity with the rule constituting that position.

A position of authority is specified for a purpose. The person who occupies the position is responsible for promoting that purpose and is allowed some discretion in the method of doing so. Further, the sphere of his power$_3$ is specified by the subject over which he may issue directives. Usually, the subject matter for directives covers all matters in which they may be needed to further the given purpose. But certain subjects may be beyond the scope of his power$_3$ even though directives on such matters might further the purpose. For example, the United States Congress may not make laws (issue directives) abridging freedom of speech. Restrictions on the subject matter of directives are substantive limits to authority. Finally, there are often specified methods for exercising power$_3$. For example, advance warning may have to be given for changes in directives. Restrictions upon the manner of issuing directives are procedural limits to authority.

The difference between *de facto* and *de jure* authority lies in the rules which constitute the authority. *De jure* authority is constituted by rules believed to be justifiable. *De facto* authority is constituted by rules which are actually operative. Of course the rules which are believed to be justifiable may also be operative. This point is illustrated by the recognition of revolutionary governments. For example, the United States government does not believe or recognize the operative rules of authority in mainland China as justifiable. But obviously many persons in mainland China and elsewhere do believe the operative rules of authority are justifiable, so the *de facto* authority is also considered *de jure* by them.

Finally, political authority must be distinguished from other kinds of authority. The distinctive feature of political authority arises from the subject matter concerning which directives may be issued. Political authority pertains to the use of the supreme coercive power$_2$ in a population or territory—usually the military or police. It may be puzzling how authority may be exercised over power$_2$ since their exercise is mutually exclusive. The key point is that authority and power$_2$ are not exercised over the same persons. This point may be illustrated by noting that while armies exercise coercive power$_2$, the structure of the army rests upon authority. An officer does not use power$_2$ to get his subordinates to carry out a task. Yet the result may be the exercise of power$_2$ over another. For a human being to wield more power$_2$ than he is physically capable of exerting by himself he must have authority over others to direct the use of their power$_2$. Hence, a person must have authority over some people in order to have power^2 over large numbers of other people.

That authority over the supreme coercive power$_2$ in a population or territory is necessary for the existence of political authority can be seen from the condition for a successful political revolution or conquest. The Chinese political revolution was over when the Communist Party under Mao Tse-tung instead of Chiang Kai-shek had supreme coercive power$_2$ over the mainland. Of course this condition only shows that Mao had *de facto* political authority. Chiang Kai-shek's claim to *de jure* political authority is the contention that he should exercise authority over the supreme coercive power$_2$ in mainland China. It must be stressed that authority over the supreme coercive power$_2$ is only a necessary condition of political authority. It may also pertain to many other subjects. However, it is always implicit that the coercive power$_2$ may be used with respect to these subjects if *de facto* authority ceases. For example, coercive power$_2$ may be used to enforce regulations of wages and hours of employment if authority fails in this area.

JUSTIFICATIONS OF POLITICAL AUTHORITY

As Professor De George so perceptively notes, the justification of authority may occur at various levels.[7] One may justify political authority in general, kinds of political authority (democratic), particular systems of political authority (the United States Constitution), or particular instances of the use of authority within that institution. These levels of justification correspond to justifying rules of various degrees of generality—rules in general, rules of a particular kind, particular rules, or the exercise of power$_3$ under these rules.

The current crisis of authority, at least with respect to political authority in the United States, has tended to move from challenging the justifiability of authority at the least general level to challenging it at a more general level. This comment only represents the trend of challenges and is not a hard and fast rule valid in all cases. But one can note a shift among young people from challenging the justification of President Johnson's intervention in Vietnam, to questioning the justification of the political system, to challenging the justification of any political authority.

It is important to be clear about the implications of denying the justifiability of political authority at any one level of generality for its justifiability at another. The unjustifiability of political authority at any level logically entails its unjustifiability at any less general level, but not at more general ones. Thus, if one denies the justifiability of the Constitution of the Commonwealth of Kentucky one denies the justifiability of all acts of political authority under that Constitution. But one does not necessarily, though one may, deny the justifiability of the Constitution of the United States. Of course the matter is much more complex than this example indicates, for one may deny the justifiability of an authority for one purpose or subject matter but not another. One may deny the justifiability of a university running an ROTC program but not its operating an agricultural extension program.

To justify authority is to provide good reasons for the rules which constitute it. The arguments concerning political obligation or authority in the sixteenth and seventeenth centuries tended to be as much concerned with what types of reasons are good ones for political authority as with the specific justification. For example, Hobbes was as concerned to deny that religious considerations are good reasons as he was to advance his own specific justification. And Locke devoted one of his *Two Treatises of Civil Government* to refuting as good reasons considerations of a religious-paternalistic sort. The most general result of this age of ferment in political philosophy was that thereafter political authority had to be justified in terms of worldly benefits to those persons subject to the authority. Religious and traditionalistic considerations were rejected. Even Burke's argument for prescription and tradition rested upon the contention that the customs evolved by a society are likely to have benefits not appreciated by rationalist thinkers.

Thus, political authority is justified in terms of its function. The function of a thing is not merely what it does, but what it does as contributing toward a purpose. The function of authority is therefore specified by filling in the purpose and subject matter in a rule constituting a position of authority. In the previous section it was shown that a necessary subject matter for political authority is the supreme coercive power$_2$ in a society. The purpose provides the justification for the use of coercion. But it may also justify issuing directives concerning more than the mere use of coercive power$_2$. Hence, the range of subject matter for political authority depends upon the purposes thought to justify the use of coercive power$_2$ as a last resort if not in the first instance. That is, justifications of political authority must show that it is either the essential or best means of furthering some purpose(s).

The limits of authority derive from its purposes as well as restrictions upon the subject matter and manner of issuing directives. Purposes provide limits in that authority is justified for furthering them, and directives are only justified to the extent that they are reasonably designed to further these purposes. Substantive and procedural limits to authority are justified by showing that furthering the given purposes is not worth the exercise of authority concerning certain matters or in certain ways. For example, freedom of religion may be justified by showing that furthering state purposes is not worth restrictions upon the exercise of religion.

Anarchists do not believe any purposes justify the establishment of authority over supreme coercive power$_2$. They believe that the purposes can be promoted without coercive power$_2$—indeed, that a society can be established in which coercive power$_2$ is never used. Defenders of political authority do not argue that the use of coercive power$_2$ is good. Indeed, they usually hope that it need not be used. But they are skeptical that society can be organized so that no one ever uses coercive power$_2$. Hence, they believe it should be under the control of authority only to be used for certain purposes.

The subjects concerning which directives may be issued are determined by the purposes of authority. Most generally, the subjects in-

clude all areas in which directives may contribute to furthering
those purposes. The more purposes a position of authority has, the
larger the number of subjects concerning which directives may be
issued. The history of Western political thought in the last three or
four centuries indicates a general increase in the number of purposes and, consequently, subjects for political authority. For Hobbes
and Locke the purposes of political authority were to provide security from violence and for economic transactions. Hobbes greatly
emphasized the security of the person, but he did not forget security
of contracts as the emerging basis of the economy. Locke somewhat
expanded the purposes of political authority by taking them to be
guaranteeing people's lives, liberty, and estates.

From the French Revolution on, two new purposes became increasingly important—justice and welfare. The French Revolution
was aimed in part at destroying the social injustice inherent in the
ancient regime. At the same time another aspect of justice was
sought by limiting political authority, e.g., the Bill of Rights of the
U.S. Constitution. Justice in this aspect does not provide a purpose
for political authority but a value not to be sacrificed in furthering
its purposes. Nonetheless, social justice as a purpose of political authority may be seen in the current movements for women's and
civil rights. Also, from the birth of socialism in the early nineteenth
century through Bismarck's welfare legislation to the twentieth
century welfare state, the role of political authority in assuring
a minimum standard of living for all has become increasingly
dominant.

The increase in the purposes of political authority has had two
major effects. First, the substantive limits to political authority
have practically vanished since fulfilling the current purposes involves regulating most aspects of social life. For example, prior to
the New Deal, political authority in the United States was limited
as to regulation of wages, hours, and many other aspects of the
economy. But once it was assumed that political authority should
assure a highly productive economy, even a Republican President
like Mr. Nixon could impose broad controls on the economy with
general public approval. Second, the use of coercive power$_2$ as a
first resort has become much less important than it was. Furthering

many of the new purposes of political authority primarily depends on expenditure of funds to encourage activities rather than restricting liberty. Nonetheless, coercive power$_2$ remains as a last resort for those who do not accept the justifiability of particular instances of the exercise of authority and for obtaining funds (taxation) to spend.

With the demise of many substantive limits to political authority, political philosophy tended to emphasize procedural matters. For example, democratic versus totalitarian forms of authority have been analyzed in depth. At a more particular level, problems of representation, due process, propaganda, and pressure groups have been the subject of much inquiry. During the decades of 1940–60 such an emphasis may have been reasonable in view of the major problems then confronting society.

But the crisis of authority arising in the last decade has resulted from questioning the purposes and subject of particular exercises of authority. The actual use of authority has been said to be unrelated to or even opposed to the purposes for which it exists. The issues of civil rights, poverty, war, and ecology emphasize the purposes of political authority. Thus, there has been much discussion of national priorities. If this analysis is correct, then the current crisis does not stem from philosophical problems about the justification of values as Professor Adams claims.[8] Indeed, one frequently finds members of the new left arguing in terms of human rights and offering naturalistic justifications of values. Rather, the crisis stems from questioning whether political authority has in fact been used to promote or hinder the purposes which justify it and whether current procedures for placing people in positions of authority result in competent people sincerely dedicated to furthering those purposes occupying the positions.

As Bertrand de Jouvenel has argued, the time has come to re-examine the purposes of political authority.[9] For it is only in terms of its purposes that the functions and limits of political authority can be justified. What is required is a detailed analysis of the purposes of political authority as justifying it with respect to different subjects.[10] Perhaps the emphasis upon purposes in the current crisis of authority will lead to such an analysis. If so, a refined and new justification of the functions and limits of political authority will evolve. Hence, the current crisis of authority may lead to its reestablishment on better understood grounds with more precisely defined functions and limits.

NOTES

1. In this volume, p. 76.

2. For a more thorough explication of this concept see section two of my paper, "A Concept of Coercion," in *Coercion: Nomos XIV*, ed. J. Roland Pennock and John W. Chapman (New York: Aldine-Atherton, 1972).

3. Whether this distinction is the same as that which De George intends by epistemic and deontic authority, I do not know. In both of my cases X primarily issues directives for Y's conduct, but if Y recognizes X as an authority he does A because he believes "Do A" is the correct judgment. It is unclear whether De George would classify this situation as an instance of epistemic authority. The case is complicated by the fact that many philosophers do not believe "Do A" can be true or false. See De George, "Epistemic Authority," p. 78ff.

4. Robert Paul Wolff, *In Defense of Anarchism* (New York: Harper and Row, 1970), p. 4.

5. See Wesley Newcomb Hohfeld, *Fundamental Legal Conceptions,* ed. Walter Wheeler Cook (New Haven: Yale University Press, 1919) pp. 35–60.

6. Cf. Joel Feinberg, "Duties, Rights and Claims," in *Law and Philosophy,* ed. Edward Allen Kent (New York: Appleton-Century-Crofts, 1970), pp. 150–51.

7. De George, "Epistemic Authority," p. 79.

8. See E. M. Adams, "The Philosophical Grounds of the Present Crisis of Authority," in this volume.

9. *Sovereignty: An Inquiry into the Political Good,* tr. J. F. Huntington (Chicago: University of Chicago Press, Phoenix Books, 1963).

10. I have attempted studies of certain purposes as justifying criminal legislation. What is required is such analyses of the jusifiability of political authority over coercive power$_2$ used as a first or last resort for all subjects and various purposes. See my "Comments: Offensive Conduct and the Law," in *Issues in Law and Morality,* ed. Norman S. Care and Thomas K. Trelogan (Cleveland: Press of Case Western Reserve University, 1973) and "Criminal Paternalism," in *Limits of Law: Nomos XV,* ed. J. Roland Pennock and John W. Chapman (New York: Lieber-Atherton, 1974).

The Functions and Limits
of Legal Authority

Wade L. Robison

Since the theory of law is a science, the basis of science proof, and the basis of proof is definition, it follows that the definition of the words "law," "more equitable," "justice" must first of all be established. That is to say, we must make clearly explicit the ideas with which we go about unwittingly judging the truth of our assertions and the correctness of the use of words.—Leibniz[1]

WHEN one is faced with a concept that is difficult to understand, a cautious method of proceeding is to examine a clear instance, preferably, "the most significant and best examples."[2] Thus we may begin to understand what it is to criticize by examining a piece of criticism—an essay, a book review. The hope of the caution is a double one. It is, first, that by beginning with an example we shall avoid theoretical assumptions or unconcious biases that might otherwise plague our enquiry at the outset. The second hope is that out of a clear case will come, as Leibniz continues, "a summary expression that will cover the cases not yet investigated."[3] I shall pursue this cautious method in regard to the concept of legal authority, but I pursue it without either hope.

For theoretical assumptions infect even the choice of examples. A policeman seems a clear case of a legal authority. He may not know much of the detail of the law and so not be the kind of legal authority a law professor may be, but he holds a position of authority within a legal system, and that ought to be enough of a characterization to get us started analyzing the sense(s) in which he is a legal authority. Yet the cautious method works only if other workers in the field accept the example as clear; and this example, however clear it may seem, is not accepted. Talcott Parsons, for example, claims that "enforcing agencies are not in a strict sense part of the legal system itself . . . at all, but are part of the political organization."[4] A policeman would thus be for Parsons a political but not a legal authority.

The example I have chosen is free from Parsons' particular objection, for I shall examine in §1 the senses in which a Supreme Court decision is legally authoritative. But as we shall see in §2, the example is not free from other objections like Parsons' which depend, as I think Parsons' does, upon theoretical difficulties in distinguishing political from legal authority. In addition, the example is problematic because the analysis I give explains and tends to confirm a curious puzzle about the status of the Court's determinations of rights, obligations, and powers. Those who think the puzzle needs a solution rather than confirmation may find something to puzzle about in my analysis. I shall begin with the puzzle.

I

Students of the Supreme Court learn early that the Court sometimes reverses itself. Some of these reversals are perceived only long after they begin, the reversal being a slow change of direction. Some are dramatically sudden: the Court sometimes directly overrules a previous decision. Law professors point these out and use them as test cases for talking about the doctrine of *stare decisis,* the the amenability of the Court to political pressure, and so on. But there is one question about such decisions that is not often raised, yet seems the most obvious of all: if the Court changes its mind about a particular legal right or power or obligation, in what sense or senses, if any, are the Court's decisions authoritative?

Let us look at a case to draw the issue more clearly. In West Virginia Board of Education v. Barnette (319 U.S. 624), the decision was that it was not lawful of a state to require as a condition for attending a public school that a pupil engage in a public flag-salute ceremony. This was in direct conflict with the Court's decision three years earlier in Minersville School District v. Gobitis (310 U.S. 586) that such a condition was lawful. We need not examine here the merits of the issue or question whether the Supreme Court was right or wrong in the second or the first decision. None of those points matter for our concerns. What matters is the problem created by the overruling for our description of the rights of the Gobitis children.

The source of the problem is that the Court was either wrong in its decision in the Gobitis case or wrong in its decision in the Barnette case. There is no way of reconciling the two decisions by distinguishing cases, limiting their range, or whatever. It was the failure of reconciliation that accounts for the Court's overruling the Gobitis case. In short, one of the two times the Supreme Court made a decision it was mistaken. The question is not which one. That is a question within the law for lawyers to argue about. The question is how to describe the rights of the defendents in the cases given that one of the decisions was wrong. For suppose that the Gobitis decision was mistaken, as the Court claimed it was. That means that if the Gobitis children had gone to court *after* the Barnette decision, they would not have been compelled to attend public school and salute the flag. But the temporal factor should make no difference to what rights or obligations they had. There had been no amendment to the Constitution since the Gobitis decision, and there had been no relevant act of Congress. There had thus been no Constitutional or statutory changes to account for the change in the Court's decision. The Court had simply made a mistake and then, against the same background of Constitutional provisions and statutory regulations, had corrected it. It seems natural to say, under the circumstances, that when the Supreme Court made its mistaken decision in the Gobitis case, the Gobitis children really did then have the legal right denied to them by the Court in that case, viz. that they attend public school without saluting the flag. This is, in fact, just what critics of the Court's decision in that case said, and the Court agreed in Barnette that they were correct. But however natural it is to say this, and despite the critics having said it and the Court's later having said it, it is also true that the Gobitis children did not have the legal right. That they did not is just what the Court decided in the Gobitis case, and the consequence of their decision was that for a number of years the children either had to go to public school and salute the flag or had to go to private school. They had the legal obligation to do one or the other, and they had it because they lost their appeal.

The problem is thus that we seem forced into the position of claiming that the Gobitis children both had a legal right to attend public school without saluting the flag and had the legal obligation to salute the flag if they attended public school. That seems hardly satisfactory, and the problem it raises about the authority of Supreme Court decisions is obvious: how can the Supreme Court be said to decide authoritatively what the rights, powers, and obligations of citizens are when as a consequence of changing its mind we know perfectly well that it has mistakenly decided that citizens have contrary rights, powers, and obligations?

A quick solution to this problem is to hold that the Court creates and extinguishes legal rights, powers, and obligations in handing down its decisions. The conflict between its decision in Gobitis and its decision in Barnette would thus be removed by pointing out that the Gobitis children had an obligation to salute the flag if they went to public school up until the time of Barnette, for the Gobitis decision created that obligation, but that because of and so as of the Barnette decision, they had no such obligation, but a right to attend public school without saluting the flag. The problem caused by the conflict between the two decisions is removed, but only at the cost of another problem: it becomes impossible to criticize the Court's decisions by referring to what they ought to have done. One cannot say, "The Supreme Court has made a mistake; what the Constitution really requires is so-and-so." For there are no independent grounds for determining what really is required: what the Court *says* in a particular case about rights or obligations *is* what the rights or obligations are. This seems unsatisfactory, for it is not descriptive of what is assumed in criticism of the Court when it hands down a controversial decision or of how the Court perceives itself. It does not claim that it is creating or extinguishing rights and obligations in making decisions. That is a legislative function. It perceives itself as adjudicating disputes and settling them by a determination of rights and obligations that are in the Constitution or in statutes. It is this perception of itself, in fact, that accounts for its *overruling* previous decisions. It would hardly need to point out and argue that it had made a mistake if it were, like a legislature, simply changing a prior state of legal relations. The Court may be deceiving itself when it does this, but if it is, it is useful self-deception. The problem it creates for the idea of the authority of Supreme Court decisions is that they seem to become divinely authoritative: the Court is perceived as God-like in its ability to create and extinguish entities, in this case legal entities—rights, powers, and obligations.

We seem to be faced with a dilemma, either horn of which seems unacceptable. For we seem compelled to claim either that the decisions of the Court are not authoritative determinations of legal rights, powers, and obligations because the Court can make (and has made) mistakes or that they are authoritative because the court can do no wrong. If we take the latter horn, we lose the ability to account for the criticism of the Court's decisions by others and, in fact, the Court's overruling its previous decision unless we put it down to wide-spread, institutionalized self-deception. If we take the former horn, we can account for the criticism of the Court's decision, but we have the problem of having to claim that while e.g. the Gobitis children had the legal right to attend public school without saluting the flag, that right had no legal effect while a contrary obligation to salute the flag if they attended public school did have legal effect. A sharpening of the dilemma and clarity about its sources rest upon distinguishing two senses in which the court's decisions are authoritative.

Understanding the first sense depends not only on an appreciation that the members of the Court are usually recognized authorities in law, but also on an understanding of the elaborate protective devices the Court employs to assure the acceptance of its decisions. These protective devices are worth laying out, however briefly, if only to indicate their scope and depth. They fall into these classes. (a) The Court has elaborate devices for screening cases brought before it on appeal. It need hear no case: there is no absolute right to be heard by the Court. And it exercises great care in its discretionary power to hear cases, sometimes rejecting a case because it is not yet ripe for adjudication, because it does not present a problem of wide enough import to justify the Court's spending time on it, because it presents an issue so political in nature that the repercussions of a decision may prevent acceptance of it and injure the perception by citizens of the Court as an independent and non-political arbiter, and on and on. (b) Once a case has been accepted for a hearing, there are devices to guarantee that the hearing is complete and fair. For instance, friends of the Court often file briefs in support of one side or the other; such briefs are welcomed. The aim is clearly to get as much information and relevant argument before the Court as possible. When a case is rejected as not ripe for adjudication, for instance, the reason just is that the issue has not raised enough of a protest or been perceived as a serious enough problem that lawyers and interest groups have taken enough of an interest in it to assure the Court that all facts and implications of the issue will be presented to it. (c) Once a case has been heard, a justice is assigned to write the majority opinion, and there is a sometimes involved and long process in which a draft opinion is circulated among the other justices by the justice assigned to write the opinion. It is some evidence of how critical the responses sometimes are that among the working papers of Justice Brandeis there is the thirty-fourth draft of one his opinions.[5]

These protective devices exist for a variety of reasons. They are protective of the Court's time, of the Court's non-political reputation, and so on. But they do have one overriding consequence: they tend to guarantee that the Court's opinion in a particular case will be perceived as reasoned both by the community-at-large and by the community of lawyers, judges, and politicians who are likely to read it closely and thus to guarantee that the Court's decision will be perceived to be reasonable. The decision's authority depends upon its being reasoned, and we may thus call this sort of authority reasoned, or "authority$_r$."[6]

It will help us to understand this sort of authority to compare and contrast it with what DE George calls epistemic authority. He contrasts epistemic authority with "the acceptance of something on the word of another."[7] This is a contrast that holds for authority$_r$ as well. For it is not the *Court's* saying that so-and-so has a right or that so-and-so does not have an obligation that makes the decision authoritative. As we shall see, the Court's decision *is* authoritative in another sense just because the Court makes it, and we can easily conceive of a judicial system in which a court's decisions were authoritative only in that sense. We need only conceive of it as being like our system except that the Supreme Court hands down decisions and never opinions to back those decisions. But our judicial system does not work that way, and because it does not, the Court's decisions are authoritative$_r$. The judges

> are conceived as lending the statutory "decisions" of an elected legis-
> lature an additional quality, by relating them to the basic principles
> of the law and thus making them authoritative. Only by fitting the
> willed statutory law in such a broader framework of "reason" does
> it become fully right, that is to say, authoritative.[8]

The judges' decisions carry weight and respect because they are (and sometimes only to the extent that they are) perceived to be reasonable in light of Constitutional constraints and statutory limits, and the Court's opinion, by giving such reasons for the decision, is meant to give the decision a sense of reasonableness.

But though reasoned authority and epistemic authority share one negative characteristic, they differ in such a way that epistemic authority might be properly construed as a sub-class of reasoned authority. De George claims that "x is an epistemic authority for y (the subject of authority) if, because of his [y's] *belief in* x's superior knowledge, y holds some proposition p, which x has enunciated (or which y believes x has enunciated), to be true or more probably true than he did before x enunciated it."[9] When one gives reasons for something, there is no necessity, however, that the reasons be for the truth (or falsity) of a proposition. For example, I may attempt to reason with my son in regard to his request for a raise in his allowance, and I may cite his failure to do all his chores, his failure to do the ones he has done properly, his lack of need for such large sums of money, and so on. All of these are reasons, how-ever good or bad, not for the truth of a proposition, but for my performing an action, the action of giving a certain amount of money every week, and for my committing myself to a rule, viz. that I shall give him so much every week.[10] In the same way, one need not conceive the Court's function in giving reasons to be to show that a particular proposition is true. The particular decision, to use J. L. Austin's barbarism, is a verdictive. It is the delivering of a finding like umpire's saying, "You're out." As such it has "obvious connexions with truth and falsity as regards soundness and un- soundness of fairness and unfairness," but in conceiving it as having those connections one *need* not conceive it as true or false, but only as being more or less reasonable.[11] A lawyer for the losing side may think the decision mistaken, but he need not deny, for all that, the authority_r of the Courts decision. He can recognize that the decision is a reasoned one and even that it is well-reasoned. If it is, he would do well to recognize it, for that will make the task of trying to get the court to change its mind and overrule the decision in some fu- ture case that much more difficult: the decision will have such authority_r, such a weight and respect, that the lawyer may find that unless he is careful in his claims and arguments his own dissents will be perceived as unreasonable by his peers and the community- at-large. It is, in short, just his acceptance of the authority of the court's decisions that will structure his dissent. There is no neces- sity, therefore, that he come to accept the court's decision as being true or more probably true in order for him to accept it as authorita- tive_r. It will be reasoned authority for him if, because of there being reasons given for it, he holds it reasonable. To put the matter somewhat formally, for any x and any y, x will be an authority_r for y, if because of y's understanding of the reasons for x, y holds x to be reasonable. This is a formulation that is defective because, al- though y ranges over *persons,* groups, and so on, x can be naturally construed as ranging only over those kinds of entities—proposi- tions, actions, rules, decisions, and so on—for which reasons are appropriate. But persons can be authorities_r as well. Making ap- propriate modifications, we can see how epistemic authority may be viewed as a sub-class of reasoned authority.[12] Some person may be a reasoned authority for someone because the reasons he gives for something show it true or more probably true; in that case he will also be an epistemic authority. But since there is no necessity that what is reasonable be true, reasoned authority is not identical with epistemic authority.

They do share one additional feature, however, that concerning the background conditions for something's being authoritative. For the Court's decision is authoritative$_r$ only if there is the possibility of coming to understand why it was given independently of the fact that the Court gave it and therefore only if there are independent grounds for the Court's decision that are accessible to all.[13] It is, in fact, just these grounds against which the Court's decision is seen to be reasonable, for those grounds are the Constitution, the sense of the law the justices have, their understanding, sometimes, of the temper of the country, and so on. They give reasons for their decision to make clear its connections with the background, to tie it up with previous decisions, and so on.

We can thus understand one way in which the authority of the Court's decisions can be limited. For the decision's authority$_r$ will be limited just to the extent that it is perceived not to be well-reasoned, not to fit in well with the Constitutional background, with previous decisions of the Court, and so on. One usual consequence are articles in law journals criticizing the decision. This is what happened in regard to the Gobitis decision, and the Court went out of its way in its decision in Barnette to recognize the articles as having had some influence in leading it to change its position. Another consequence is that lawyers hesitate to use the case as a precedent. This is what happened in regard to Betts v. Brady (316 U.S. 455), for that decision, concerning the rights of indigents to counsel in state criminal trials, was perceived to be out-of-step with the general tenor of the Court's opinions regarding the due-process clause of the Fourteenth Amendment. They were right to be hesitant. The case was eventually overruled in Gideon v. Wainwright (372 U.S. 335).

But the appeal to an independent background against which to criticize the Court's decisions and to accept them as being authoritative$_r$ has a consequence for the dilemma we examined. Since to claim that the Court's decisions are authoritative$_r$ is to commit oneself to the claim that there are independent grounds upon which the Court's decisions can be judged, we cannot accept that the Court simply creates or extinguishes rights and obligations by the very act of deciding: it sometimes makes mistakes and those mistakes are mistakes just because the Supreme Court says that an obligation or right exists (or does not exist) when there are compelling reasons for saying it does not (or that it does). An examination of this sense of authority thus removes one horn of the dilemma, for it is true that the Court's decisions are authoritative$_r$.

But before we conclude that the other horn of the dilemma is the correct one, we should examine the other sense in which the decisions of the Court are authoritative. We may call this sense "authoritative$_a$" for "authoritative determination." For J. L. Austin is right: decisions are verdictives. They are the deliverings of findings, and the findings are determinations of a person's (or a corporation or any other legal entity capable of having rights, obligations, or powers) legal relations. That is, they determine that the person has or does not have a right, an obligation, or a legal power. For example, if someone is found guilty of breaking a criminal law and loses his appeal that the law is unconstitutional, he is properly described as "guilty of a crime." The Court has decided that he does not have the legal right to do what he did, and the consequence is that his legal relations are other than what he claims them to be: he is a criminal. If he should bolt upon hearing the decision, a policeman would take the Court's decision as sufficient authorization to pick him up. In short, the Court's decision is authoritative simply because it determines legal rights, obligations, and powers.

It is not because it is the Supreme Court making the decision that the decision is authoritative$_a$. That the court is the Supreme Court only means that the decision is the last that the defendant is entitled to within our judicial process. The decision is authoritative$_a$ because it is a court that is making it. This is something that is authoritative simply because of a *court's saying* so-and-so. Both the "saying" and "a court" need to be italicized. It is the decision itself that determines the rights, obligations, or powers, and it it a court's making that decision that makes the determination authoritative.

An analogy may make this clearer. If it is the habit of a family to go bicycling every Sunday afternoon and if there are disagreements about where to bicycle, it may be decided to rotate the decision among the members of the family so that one decides one week, the next the next, and so on. If there is then a disagreement about where to go, it is the saying where to go of the person whose turn it is to decide that is decisive. He need give no reasons, and authority$_d$ is thus distinguished from authority$_r$. His decision will be authoritative provided that the family has agreed upon a certain decision-procedure and that procedure is being followed. The person's decision is thus authoritative because it accords with the rules governing how decisions are to be made and it is authoritative for those persons who have accepted those rules.[14]

Transporting this homely example to the setting of the Supreme Court requires stretching the sense of acceptance employed in order to account for the effect the Court's decisions have. But in whatever stretched sense, acceptance of the Court's decisions does occur. The Court actually makes a decision only about a particular case: it decides that the *Gobitis* children do not have the right to attend public school without saluting the flag. The normal consequence of a decision, however, is that other children, who did not go to Court at all, are also obligated to attend school under the condition and that various states and school districts take action, on the basis of the Court's decision in the particular case, to insure compliance in other cases. This is the normal consequence just as it is the normal consequence that the losing party in the particular case does what the Court has determined it has a legal obligation to do or ceases to do what the Court has determined it has no legal right to do. These normal consequences occur when the Court's decision has been accepted by the parties involved, by executive and lower judicial officials of Federal, State, and local governments, who, because of that acceptance, are willing to enforce the decision, and by others who are not willing to take their cases to court because they judge the odds against winning now too long to make it worth their while. For example, though the Court's recent decision regarding the death penalty applied only to the law in one state and though there was a great outcry in some states regarding the decision, no other state has attempted to continue using the death penalty in just the way in which the Court decided the one state could not.

The consequence of the acceptance of the Court's decision is then normally not simply the settlement of a dispute in a particular case, but the settlement of it in such a way that the settlement permeates the political system so that similar cases are handled in

similar ways without the need for a case by case review. But this is
not just a consequence. It is the function of the Court to settle disputes in this way. It need not be, for one can imagine a system in
which the judiciary settles disputes case by case and not, as it were,
institutionally. But in our system the function of the Court is to
settle particular disputes when they come to the point where the
parties disputing cannot reach agreement and to settle those particular disputes in such a way that the principles of settlement permeate the rest of the system. The former function is served by
the Court's authority$_a$. Its saying, "This is how things are," is sufficient to settle particular disputes given that the parties to the
dispute accept its authority to decide and its decision was procedur-
ally correct. But its authority$_a$ has the wider effect of setting the
principles for settling similar disputes because of the Court's authority. There is nothing in the authority of a particular decision
that requires that other parties who may wish to dispute the issue
not dispute it: they are not legally bound by that particular decision
to do what the Court says the particular parties to the dispute must
do. Their acceptance of the principles that settle that particular dispute, or their acceptance that others accept these principles, binds
themselves, and the crucial condition necessary for that acceptance
is that the Court give reasons for its particular decision. Those reasons make the decision a principled one. In short, the Court's au-
thority$_r$ is a condition for its authority$_a$ having the institutional
effects it has. For those who accept its authority$_a$, its giving reasons
for its decisions makes it *prima facie* unreasonable for them and
others to refuse to go along with principles of settlement.

When I speak of the authority *simpliciter* of the Court's decisions, I mean both their authority$_a$ and authority$_r$. They are tied together into a single sense of authority because of the single complex
function the Court has. But that authority is limited in two different ways corresponding to the two components of the Court's
function. On the one hand someone may not think the Court's decision authoritative because he refuses to accept the Court as the
proper body to make decisions regarding disputes; or because, accepting that, he refuses to accept that the Court has followed the
proper procedure in coming to a decision; or because, accepting the
Court as the proper body and its procedure in deciding as correct, he

refuses to accept the Court's decision in a particular case. The last possibility is most easily envisaged for someone who holds there is an overriding moral reason for not doing what he would agree he was otherwise legally obligated to do. The authority of the Court's decision is so limited because the person in question is not accepting the authority$_d$ of the Court or, accepting it, is not accepting it as authoritative for non-legal (e.g. moral) problems as well as legal ones. But the authority of the Court's decisions is also limited to the extent that its decisions are not perceived to have authority$_r$. When the Court's decision, as in Gobitis, is not perceived as fitting in with its previous decisions or with the more permanent values embodied in the Constitution, the decision calls forth articles of criticism and, sometimes, overruling either by the Court itself or by the Congress.

This brings us back to the problem with which we began: how can the Court's decisions be authoritative when it can make (and has made) mistakes in determining rights, obligations, and powers? We can now see that so long as the Court is accepted as an arbiter of disputes, its decisions are authoritative$_d$ even when it does make mistakes. But given that they are also authoritative$_r$ (though they may be more or less so), we are back with the problem in its full-force: we seem compelled to say sometimes both that someone has e.g. a legal obligation to do something because the Court has decided that he does and that he has a legal right not to do what they decided he must do because the Court has misconstrued what the Constitution or laws require. The source of this compulsion is to be found, I suggest, in the complex function of the Court. It must make decisions in particular cases so that even when it makes mistakes, it has made an authoritative determination, and since it must attempt to make the principles of settlement permeate the system, it invites criticism of that determination by the very attempt to make it authoritative not simply for the particular case, but also for similar cases. If it made authoritative determinations and could give no reasons in terms of the Constitutional and legal background conditions, there would be no foothold for mistakes. If it gave Constitutional and statutory reasons for settling a matter one way or the other, but determined no particular settlement, there would be no sense of conflict between its giving poor reasons and its authoritatively determining rights, obligations, and powers. But it has the function of settling particular disputes institutionally. There is, therefore, I think, no solution to the problem. One may attempt to get out of the immediate difficulty by talking of competing *claims* to rights or obligations, one backed by the Court's decision and the other by a reasoned case drawn from the Constitution, and so on. But that simply obscures the difficulty: there just are cases where one has to say that the Court has authoritatively determined that e.g. someone has a legal obligation and yet that he does not have that legal obligation. Such an ending is an unhappy one for those who like their ontologies neat, but the legal system is not for tidy ontologies. It is for certain ends, and there is nothing one can do to alleviate the sense of conflict except to explain that it has its source in the complex function of the Court.

II

A sufficient reason for lacking hope that we would find "a summary expression that will cover the cases not yet investigated" is that the authority of the decisions of the Supreme Court is not a kind of authority that one much finds, or would expect to find, elsewhere in a political system. It is one of the features of the decision's being authoritative that there is only *one* body making such decisions. One may check the quasi-courts in administrative agencies or examine the sense in which the decisions of lower courts are authoritative, but that will leave us with little to go on to investigate the sense, for example, in which a policeman is a legal authority. His decisions are clearly not authoritative in the sense in which a court's decisions are. It is not his function to settle disputes.

One may respond that a policeman is not a legal authority: after all, we have a definitive case in Court decisions, and policemen just do not match up. But this response assumes that a Court's decisions are legally authoritative and that Parson's is the correct solution to the problem of distinguishing legal from political authority. But neither of these assumptions is justified. I have explained in §1 in what senses the Court's decisions are authoritative, but not in what sense they are legally so, and, not having done that, I have made no assumptions about how to distinguish legal from political authority.

The theoretical difficulties involved in the latter can be probed by examining Michael Bayles' claim that "the distinctive feature of political authority arises from the subject matter concerning which directives may be issued."[15] This does not say what it may at first sight seem to say. Bayles is not saying that there is a peculiar subject matter, like economic activity or the welfare of persons, which is, unlike religious pronouncements and morality, the distinct province of political authority. Such a claim, if not stipulative, would be false, for it is easy to find examples of political authorities that issue directives concerning matters of religion, morals, or what have you. A church-state is such an example. The "subject-matter" Bayles has in mind is rather what he calls "the supreme coercive power, in a population or territory" where by "power" is meant an ability to affect another's behavior through intending to reward or punish.[16] What makes something a distinctly political authority for Bayles is thus not what subject-matter it may issue directives about, as his formulation suggests, but whether its directives are backed by such a power. Bayles' definition looks antipositivistic because it seems to impose some limits on the subject matter of political authority, but in fact he is in essential agreement with John Austin's positivist characterization of political authority. For Austin there can be positive law, and so a legal system, only if there is a sovereign, i.e. a political authority, some individual or set of individuals, who owes no duty to any other political authority, but who is habitually obeyed by the bulk of the citizens.[17] Such a definition makes political authority unlimited in what it is authoritative over and, more to our point, makes it a necessary condition for legal authority.

And it is: given certain contingent features of human beings, such as the recalcitrance of some, it is necessary to back laws (and judicial decisions) with power not simply to have an efficient working legal system, but to have any legal system at all. But to distinguish legal authority from political authority one then seems inexorably led either to slice off part of the political system (e.g., the non-enforcing agencies) as being distinctly legal or to take the legal system as a way of exercising political authority. Parsons does the former, and Austin does the latter, treating law as an efficient way of affecting behavior.

If one takes Parsons' route, there is a problem about examples because individuals who are political authorities are not legal authorities, and if one takes Austin's route, there is a problem because all individuals who are legal authorities are also political authorities. In either case the example I have chosen is a problematic one. If Austin is correct and we should look upon laws as an efficient way in which political authority is exercised, then in explaining how the decisions of the Supreme Court are authoritative, I have done nothing to explain in what way they are legally authoritative as distinct from being politically authoritative. But in explaining how the Court's decisions are authoritative in a unique way, in such a way as to give no "summary expression" for such examples as policemen, I appear already to have committed myself to Parsons' general move that he would look upon the judiciary as the essentially legal part of a state since it can be clearly demarcated from the enforcing (power-using) parts. In short, the question of whether we have got in Supreme Court decisions an example of a legal authority and the question of what makes them legally authoritative hinge upon a prior determination of the difference between political and legal authorities. One cannot work from cases in an attempt to discover the difference; the difference must be settled first.

Settling the difference is a matter not simply of descriptive accuracy and adequacy, but also of such other factors as, for example, moral import. If Parsons is correct and a policeman is not a legal authority, we lose an important moral hold upon his actions. For the word "legal" carries in its ordinary use the connotation of legitimate, a connotation which gives a standard for evaluation that "political" does not. Though I shall not argue the point in this paper, one obvious objection to Parsons' move is that it commits one to the false claim that judges do not enforce the law.[18] My own view is that we should settle the difference by making Austin's general move: political authorities find it a matter of practical necessity to operate through laws.[19] A legal authority is thus also a political authority, and a political authority is not a legal authority only when in characterizing the authority we have no essential recourse to laws or Constitutional principles. For example, a President's calling a foreign minister to congratulate him on his government's

128 W. L. ROBISON

actions or console him for his country's disasters is an action of the President, but of the President as a political authority: there is no law or Constitutional provision relevant to characterizing such a call, though there are good political reasons for making it.

The decisions of the Court are legally authoritatve both because of the kinds of reasons it cites to make its decisions authoritative$_r$ and because of the nature of the conditions necessary for its decisions being authoritative$_a$. The kinds of reasons cited are, in short, legal reasons—Constitutional principles, previous statutes, "the aim of the law," and so on. It does not take an astute observer of the political system to realize that the Court has sometimes made the particular determinaton it has because of what can only be described as what it perceives as political necessity. But the Court does not cite political factors in its decisions. Its function is to make even those decisions which are poltically necessitated reasonable in terms of Constitutional and statutory provisions. The conditions necessary for its decisions being authoritative$_a$ are also legal. The Court is itself a legal entity, created by law and Constitutional provisions, and it operates under legally regulated procedures. These facts about the Court are as important as that it appeals to the Constitution and statutes in making decisions: making determinations of rights, powers, and obligations would not be legal if it were unguided by statutory restraints and Constitutional principles, and the Court's making those determinations would not make them legally authoritative if it did not follow established procedure and were not itself created by the law. It is acceptance of the laws and rules regulating its decision-making that accounts for the acceptance of the Court as authorized to make decisions. What makes the authority of the Court a legal authority is thus that its authority$_a$ and authority$_r$ are both backed, though in different ways, by law and Constitutional provisions.

One may object that this explanation of what makes an x legally authoritative is defective because it appeals essentially to law. It is this objection that in part lies behind my having no hope that a summary expression of what makes something a legal authority could come from investigating particular cases: the examples one picks as examples of legal authority are determined to be such examples because of a prior commitment to some theory of legal authority. In short, theories are themselves authoritative in determining what count as examples of what they are theories of. At best, therefore, I have explained, on the assumption of a theory about legal authority, *how* Supreme Court decisions are legally authoritative. To give such a pathology of Court decisions is not unhelpful: we know enough to know that theories are not authoritative in just the ways in which the Courts decisions are. But whether the theory I assume should be accepted is another question. If it is accepted, one must accept that a policeman is a legal authority. He is both because in making determinations of whom to arrest he is supposed to be guided by law and because he has met the conditions established by law for being a policeman. On my view, that is, the political system of which the Court is a part is permeated by legal authorities. I think this both accurate and good, but I should not like my view accepted on the basis of my saying so. There are reasons for my saying so, and they need to be stated if my saying so is to be authoritative.

NOTES

1. "Elements of Law and Equity," in Phillip P. Weiner, editor, *Leibniz Selections,* Charles Scribner's Sons (New York: 1951), pp. 1–2.

2. Ib*id.,* p. 2.

3. *Ibid.*

4. "Authority, Legitimation, and Political Action," in Carl J. Friedrich, editor, *Authority,* Harvard Univ. Press (Cambridge, Mass.: 1958), p. 214.

5. Anthony Lewis, *Gideon's Trumpet,* Vintage Book (New York: 1964), p. 183.

6. See in regard to this sense of authority Carl J. Friedrich's excellent article, "Authority, Reason, and Discretion," in *Authority, op. cit.,* pp. 28–48. That there is such a sense of authority runs counter to the common assumption that e.g. a person who "gives his reasons . . . is not functioning as an authority. He functions as an authority when he states his *ipse dixit."* (Jerome Hall, "Authority and the Law," in *Authority, op. cit.,* p. 63. See also in this regard, R. S. Peters, "Authority," *Aristotelian Society Proceedings, Supplement,* 1958, pp. 217–19.)

7. Richard T. De George, "The Nature and Function of Epistemic Authority," in this volume, p. 93.

8. Friedrich, *op. cit.,* p. 31.

9. Ibid., p. 91. Though De George introduces this as "a formal definition of *de facto* epistemic authority" (*Ibid.*, p. 90), he clearly does not
intend it to be taken in quite the rigorous way his introduction may lead
one to think. For example, one can be an epistemic authority not simply
for the truth, but also for the falsity of a proposition. In addition, De
George's formulation is natural for an authority who is a person or group
of persons, but as he goes on to say, x may be "a text or other written work
or document," and so on (*Ibid.*, p. 91). What is thus needed to have a
formal definition is some more general formula in which the language itself does not necessitate a certain sort of instantiation and does not prevent
epistemic authorities from being authorities only for the truth of propositions. I am sure De George recognizes this, but since I shall be contrasting
my own conception of how Supreme Court *decisions* are authoritative$_r$
with De George's conception of how an x can be epistemically authoritative, it is worth pointing this out so as not to become entangled in purely
verbal differences.

10. I am assuming here that to attempt to convert such actions and rules
to propositions capable of being true and false would not only distort what
we in fact do when we sometimes give reasons, but would distort them in
such a way as to have unfortunate consequences for our understanding of
authority. I shall not argue the point here except to say that *if* one holds
that decisions can be true or false, the problem with which we began this
section becomes that much more difficult to handle.

11. J. L. Austin, *How to do things with Words,* ed. J. O. Urmson,
Clarendon Press (Oxford: 1962), p. 152.

12. The formulation given is a sufficient condition for something's
being a *de facto* authority$_r$. Another formulation more natural for x's
being a person is that for any x and y, x will be authority$_r$ for y, if, because of y's understanding of x's reasons for some z (where z is a decision,
proposition, etc.), y holds z to be more reasonable.

13. See De George, *Ibid.*, p. 93.

14. See Theodore M. Benditt, "Authority and Authorization," this volume, p. 5. Benditt gives an example like the one I have given, but in regard
to another issue, viz. how autonomy and authority can be reconciled.

15. Michael Bayles, "The Functions and Limits of Political Authority,"
this volume, p. 105.

16. *Ibid.*, pp. 106 and 102.

17. John Austin, *The Province of Jurisprudence Determined,* ed. H. L.
A. Hart, Weidenfeld and Nicolson (London: 1954), p. 202. One difference between Austin's conception and Bayles' is that obedience for Austin
comes only through fear of a sanction, whereas for Bayles the authority

has power$_2$ in that harms *or rewards* are intended. I do not take this to be a crucial difference.

18. I owe this point to Wallace Anderson.

19. See H. L. A. Hart, *The Concept of Law,* Clarendon Press (Oxford: 1961), p. 21.

The Function and
Limits of
Religious Authority

R. Baine Harris

OF THE four main historical types of authority: civil, moral, scientific (epistemic), and religious, the last one has received the greatest challenge in modern times. Numerous historical and social factors are involved in this challenge, not the least of which is the widespread difference of opinion concerning the *meaning* of religious authority itself. In this paper I shall explore some of the usages of the term as it has been understood in the West and propose a more precise definition. I shall take the postion that religious authority is not reduceable to any of the other three types and that it is both meaningful and viable when properly defined .

I

The major ideological source of the notion of religious authority in the West is the Old Testament, the one document that has contributed significantly to the formation of the basic religious, moral, and legal notions of the Judaic, Christian, and Islamic tradtions. The book of Genesis teaches that all forms of authority rest ultimately in religious authority. On the assumption that ultimate rights inhere in the ultimate source, it teaches that God has authority over man because He is his Creator. He is his *Author!* In Ancient Israel the father was believed to be the total biological source of his offspring, since his sperm was thought to be a complete individual that only grew within the womb. This belief is likely the basis for the bias toward male supremacy in the Old Testament and the view that a man's children are his own property. Throughout the whole of the Old Testament, the "Word of the Lord" is final, and the assumption that religious authority should predominate over all other forms prevails.

The Old Testament is also a major source of the confusion of the meaning of religious authority. In the Patriarchs and in Moses we find not only the priority of religious authority over the other forms but also the coalescence of all four forms into one office or one man. Moses' religious authority rested in the fact that he spoke for Jehovah—he spoke the Word of the Lord—but he also exercised civil, moral, and epistemic authority as well. In his case the implication is clear that his authenticity as a representative of Jehovah formed the basis of his moral, civil, and epistemic authority. With the rise of Joshua and the Judges there was the beginning of the separation of the four forms, since Josuah's authority was probably more civil and epistemic than it was religious. By the time of King Saul and King David, civil authority clearly prevailed over religious authority. Later Old Testament history can be seen as a conflict between the four forms of authority, namely, a debate as to which form should prevail over the others. By the time of the later prophets, religious authority was effectively divorced from civic authority and there arose a new kind of religious authority, the religious expert whose expertise was confined to strictly religious and moral issues.

To some extent the history of Western Europe parallels the history of Ancient Israel in this respect, moving from the centering of all forms of authority in the religious leader to the establishment of each form on its own basis. Although the Islamic cultures generally kept civil and religious authority together, the Christian West often battled to keep them apart. The exact function of religious authority was never settled in the Christian West and disagreement over it has been one of the causes of civil strife.

Essentially, there have been three different issues in the West that have led to the confusion concerning the meaning of the concept "religious authority." The first is the battle to separate civil, moral, and scientific authority from any dependency upon a religious base. The second is the conflict between the Church and the State for the control of society. The third is the debate that has gone on within the various religious circles concerning the criteria that should be used in the authenticating of religious meaning. I shall now discuss each one of these briefly.

A relgous society is one in which religious sanctions finally apply. In a theistic context this means that God is the final judge —that all matters—civil, moral, scientific, or whatever, must eventually come "under God." As I see it, both in the Old Testament and the history of Europe there is an effort to maintain an essentially theistic religious society while allowing civil, moral, and scientific authority to have their own groundings apart from religious authority. The rise of the state, the development of the sciences, and the establishment of morality on a non-religious base have all been accomplished only through challenging the limits to which religion and religious meanings are allowed to apply. We also notice that both in the Old Testament and in the history of Western Europe a dynamic tension exists between the "religous" and secular forces and further suggest that much of the friction results from difference of opinions concerning just how far religious authority should apply. Generally speaking, the solution to the conflict has been to produce a more narrow definition of religious authority, namely, one that restricts religious meanings to those not involving the state or morality or science.

The conflict between the established religious and civil authorities in the West has been, in the main, a battle to gain performatory authority over society rather than a direct challenge to the validity of the other type of authority. It has often led to controversies over the range of religious authority and even to the claim of the absolute priority of one type over the other. In Rome under the Caesars, for example, the priority of civil authority was clearly established, but with the emergence of the Christian Church as a political force and the establishment of the Holy Roman Empire, the priority of religious authority was asserted. Luther and the Lutheran Protestants generally followed the Ockhamistic view that civil and religious authority must be separate, and even conceivably equal, whereas the Calvinists opted in favor of stronger religious authority. The Anglicans, accepting neither of these positions, worked out a formula whereby the Church becomes an element of civil authority. The Anabaptists, Jews, Quakers, and Free Churchmen have objected to all the above positions, affirming only the independent character of religious authority. It now appears that the battle has been won by the State in most Western Nations, since the State now usually has effective performatory authority over society.

Historically, there have been three final appeals in the verification of religious authority: religious experience, scripture, and religious tradition. Of these three, religious experience is the most significant. The three major religious traditions of the West are based upon the religious experience of their founder, or founders, and it is that experience that is preserved in sacred scripture and hopefully passed on to future generations through an authentic tradition. In addition, the three traditions have also had mystics who rely more upon their *own* religious experience than they do upon scriptures or historic traditions. Thus, a three-way battle for the validation of religious authorty arises between those who rely on scriptures, traditions, and personal experience as the final guide for religious meanings. Even the term "religious expert" is confused and ambiguous, for it is not clear whether the expert is an expert in interpreting scriptures and traditions or in having or explaining religious experiences.

II

The above presentation should serve to illustrate the difficulty in coming up with any one unequivocal meaning of the term "religious authority" based upon its historical usage. We now propose a stipulative defintion of Representative Religious Authority; but before doing so, some further distinctions must be made. The first is between genuine religious authority and *de facto* religious authority, conceding that the two are not necessarily mutually exclusive. At issue is what it means to exercise religious authority! Does it mean to be religiously authorative or authoritatively religious? It would be possible to serve in the capacity of a religious authority, that is, to function as an authority for religion, without actually being religiously authentic. A *de facto* religious authority may serve all the formal functions of an authority for religion while not possessing a *religious* force. The line between the true prophet and the false prophet has always been very fine.

The second distinction that must be made is between the exercise of religious authority as religious authority and its exercise as a form of civil, moral, or epistemic authority. There have been numerous instances of individuals who have professed to exercise religious authority whereas in fact they have used this claim as a basis for exercising some form of civil or moral epistemic authority. Conversely, there have also been instances of persons who have professed to be exercising some form of civil, moral, or epistemic authority when they have actually exercised religious authority.

Further differentiation must also be made between (1) Ultimate Religious Authority, such as God or Brahmin and (2) Representative Religious Authority, such as a religious individual or a church who "stands for" ultimate religious authority. Most historcal instances of religious authority have been the latter. Neither form would apply in atheistic societies, but in theistic societies it is recognized that some final authority stands over and above any functional religious authority. In the latter God is *in* authority but not *an* authority, and it would not be significant to speak of him as a religious authority. Generally speaking, when "religious authority" is used in theistic societies it is "representative religious authority" that is intended, since the issue is not whether God is *an* authority, but who speaks authoritatively for God.

Representative Religious Authority. We now propose the following definition of Representative Religious Authority: "Y may be said to have religious authority over X if X is convinced that Y is the correct representative of the deity or has the power of the ultimate force or forces of the universe representatively embodied in him to some degree." If this is the case. Y exercises a force over X, but the nature and extent of that force is determined more by X than it is by Y. This force operates only with the consent of X and it is determined more by the opinions and judgments of X about Y than it is by Y's own opinions and judgments about himself. It is possible for Y not even to be aware of the fact that he is exercising a force over X or even not to be aware of X's existence.

The force that Y exercises over X is a sacred force, i.e., it is exclusively religious. It applies only to distinctly religious meanings and sanctions and refers only to the highest ideals and values of X's religion. Ultimately, it refers beyond Y to the force of the deity that Y is believed to represent, and in this sense it becomes an extension of the deity in the minds of X. Y's own religious opinions and his own view of his religious authority are not directly relevant, since it is X's conclusion that Y is the *bona fide* representative of the deity that is important and not, strictly speaking, Y's own knowledge.

It follows from the above definition that Y's most important quality is his capacity to be transparent to the deity. His genius rests not in his originality, his knowledge, or his own personal moral character, but in his *de facto* embodiment of those ideals and values approved by the deity (or believed to be approved by the deity.) He is innocent in the sense of being completely devoted to God's purposes. His single most important characteristic is his capacity to be open to God. (cf. Samuel, the Virgin Mary, Jesus, St. Paul, Mohammed, and Vivekananda.) It is often the case that in his naive single mindedness he is not at all aware of the fact that he is exercising a force over anyone else.

Although there is no theoretical reason why the same individual cannot exercise religious and political authority simultaneously, it does not follow that the two can be merged into one. If by civil authority we mean that the locus of power resides ultimately in the will of the body politic, we can easily see its incompatibility with representative religious authority, since the former is essentially a public determination while the latter is a private one. The election to be the representative of the *vox populi* does not qualify one to be the *vox deus,* or *vice versa.* As Professor Bayles indicates, to have authority over conduct is not necessarily to have authority over belief.[1] In civil or political authority, the right to act is based upon rules instituted by those over which the authority is exercised, so that the authority of the ruler is in the rules, and not, strictly speaking, in the ruler. In representative religious authority, on the other hand, the locus of the authority is in the representative of the deity.

In those instances in which an attempt has been made to merge the two forms into one person or government or society, the situation has usually not worked out very well. Very often the individual becomes confused about his rights in his dual roles and claims the wrong sanctions for his action. In most cases the result has been the secularization of religious authority, which by our definition is the same as its loss.

By the above definition, religious authority cannot be a form of moral authority, or *vice versa,* although, again there is no reason why the two cannot be simultaneously embodied in the same individual. As Professor Werkmeister suggests, moral authority must be based upon *principles* which are unchallengeable.[2] It rests upon ontologically justifiable normative ideals, and as such is not cognitive and epistemically derived.[3] The main difference between it and religious authority as we have defined it is that it has its force in consensus whereas the latter does not.

Moral authority cannot be a form of religious authority, since there is no way of moving from the sort of persuasion that Y has over X to a universal appeal. Moral authority must apply universally and no such universal claims could ever be made on the basis of religious authority as we have defined it. Religious authority is typically vested in persons rather than in principles and its ideals and values are individually orientated. The only cases we can imagine when the two forms can function together is in dealing with religious issues that have moral significance or moral issues that have religious significance; but then the one applies independently of the other.

One of the reasons for the frequent confusion of these two forms is the fact that those who exercise *de facto* religious authority very often attempt to exercise moral authority as well. The Pope often appeals to moral authority, as do Presidents and Generals as well. But according to our definition, there can be no *de jure* moral authority established on the basis of religious authority, if, indeed, there can be any *de jure* moral authority at all. There would not be any inconsistency, however, in the same individual exercising the charismatic function necessary to the development of moral authority while at the same time serving as a religious authority for someone.

The final question remaining is whether religious authority can be a form of epistemic authority. Is the saint merely an expert on religious knowledge? The answer depends upon the connotation allowed to the notion "epistemic." If it is restricted to authority based upon knowledge, the answer should be negative; whereas if the term is expanded to cover anyone who has some influence over another person by virtue of his superior ability or character or behavior, the response should likely be positive. Clearly Y is an authority for X and this is based upon some judgment by X of Y's expertness in religious affairs. This judgment, however, is not based upon Y's knowledge alone, but refers to his general character. Y's expertness must be his expertness in representing the deity, and this could hardly be labeled a skill, a science, or an artistic accomplishment. In fact, in the Old Testament the point is usually made that *God* chose a specific individual to be his representative without his own consent and often in spite of his lack of talents. (cf. Jonah, Jeremiah, Amos)

A sage, prophet, theologian, or holy man may be regarded as a religious expert; but by our definition, only the holy man is a religious authority, since only he "stands for" the deity. A sage is an epistemic religious authority. His expertness is the product of learning and wisdom about religious issues. The prophet often speaks for God, but he does not necessarily exhibit or embody the nature of the God he speaks for. A theologian is a "God-scientist," an expert on the nature of deity; and as such his authority is that of a scientist. It is epistemic rather that religious.

In summary, religious authority is a force that one individual holds over another individual in virtue of the latter's opinion that the former is a true representative of the deity. It is personal and deontic and incapable of objective verification. It is *de facto* and usually effective and informal. It has no direct extension into civil, moral, or epistemic issues, except to the extent that those issues have a purely religious element involved in them. The establishment of religious authority carries with it no inherent civil, moral, or epistemic rights, just as the establishment of the other three forms of authority carry no inherent religious rights.

The breakdown in respect for religious authority is one of the factors contributing to much of the current unrest in our society. Some religious authorities have been partly responsible for this loss of respect by insisting upon extending religious sanctions into areas in which they do not apply. The return to respect for religious authority can be effected, we believe, by a closer restriction of its domain and by its own inner reformation and purification.

NOTES

1. See pp. 101–102 of this volume.
2. See pp. 97–98.
3. See p. 99.

Authority:
A Bibliography

Richard T. De George

IF authority is taken in a broad sense, the literature concerned with it is enormous. In order to keep this bibliography within manageable limits, therefore, I have had to draw a somewhat arbitrary line in deciding what to include and what to omit. (1) I have given preference to the philosophical literature dealing with authority. (2) Though this bibliography contains a considerable number of items dealing with authority in religion or with the authoritarian personality or with sociological studies on authority in different societies, I have frequently omitted entries on these topics, especially where the items were very short, or by a relatively unknown author publishing in an obscure journal. (3) I have given preference to more recent works and have included very few items which were published before 1900. (4) I have listed chapters dealing with authority in books on other topics but since these are especially difficult to track down, I can make no claim to completeness. (5) There is a large literature dealing with civil disobedience, anarchy, and similar topics; in general I have had to ignore these topics, and I have restricted my entries to those works which deal more directly with authority as such. (6) Because of the criteria I have used, there are very few references to discussions of authority in works by giants in the history of philosophy. This is because very few of the classical philosophers have written works or chapters dedicated specifically

141

to authority. (7) There are a number of works which contain collections of papers or symposia on authority. To list all of the contributions to these volumes separately would have been to extend my already long list to intolerable lengths. I have therefore simply mentioned the contributors, or the more prominent among them, in a note following the volume in question. (8) Finally, I have noted within my bibliography a number of books which themselves contain bibliographies. Although many of the items which I list also appear in those bibliographies, the latter are sometimes more complete when dealing with disciplines other than philosophy, and they frequently cite books and articles which fall outside of the selection criteria I have employed.

ADAMS, P., J. SCHWAB and J. APONTE. "Authoritarian Parents and Disturbed Children," *American Journal of Psychiatry*, CXXI (1965), 1162-1167.

ADORNO, T .W. [and others]. *The Authoritarian Personality*. New York: Science Editions, 1964. 2v. [Originally published, Harper, 1950.] Bibliog: pp. 977-982.

ALFIERI, V. E. *Autorità e libertà nelle moderne teorie della politica*. Milano: Marzorati, 1947, 279 p.

ARENDT, H. "Authority in the Twentieth Century," *Review of Politics*, XVIII (1956), 403-17.

ARENDT, H. "What is Authority?" in her *Between Past and Future: Six Exercises in Political Thought*. New York: The Viking Press, 1954.

"AUTHORITY AND FREEDOM," *Church Quarterly Review*, CLV (1954), 214-215.

"AUTHORITY AND FREEDOM," by the Warden of All Souls. *Spectator*, CLV (1935), 854-5.

"AUTHORITY AND FREEDOM: SYMPOSIUM," *Blackfriars*, XXI (1940), 563-619. [Includes articles by B. Delany, V. McNebb, B. Magentry, G. Vann, K. Foster, I. Thomas, and C. Pepler.]

"AUTHORITY IN THE CHRISTIAN CHURCH," *Modern Churchman*, XXIII (1933), 283-356. [Includes articles by J. S. Bezzant, J. M. Creed, G. L. H. Harvey, and M. T. Dunlop.]

"L'AUTORITÀ NELLA CHIESA," *La Civiltà Cattolica*, CXX (1969), 417-423.

AXINN, S. "Kant, Authority, and the French Revolution," *Journal of the History of Ideas*, XXXII (1971), 423-32.

BAIER, K. "The Justification of Governmental Authority," *Journal of Philosophy*, LXIX (1972), 700-16.

BANTOCK, G. H. *Freedom and Authority in Education: A Criticism of Modern Cultural and Educational Assumptions.* 2d ed. London: Farber, 1965. 212 p.

BARBEY, L. "Contestation et autorité pédagogique," *Civitas*, XXIV (1969), 703-710.

BARKER, E. "Corporate Authority and Its Sanctions," *Modern Churchman*, XIX (1929), 300-12.

BARKER, E. N. "Authoritarianism of the Political Right, Center, and Left," *Journal of Social Issues*, XIX (1963), 63-74.

BARNARD, F. M. "The 'Practical Philosophy' of Christian Thomasius," *Journal of the History of Ideas*, XXXII (1971), 221-46.

BARTOLINI, L. *Della sottomissiane.* Roma: OET, 1945. 87 p.

BASS, B. M. "Authoritarianism or Acquiescence?" *Journal of Abnormal and Social Psychology*, LI (1955), 616-23.

BATES, S. "Authority and Autonomy," *Journal of Philosophy*, LXIX (1972), 175-76.

BAYLES, M.D. "In Defense of Authority," *Personalist*, LII (1971), 755-59.

BAYS, D. H. "The Nature of Provincial Political Authority in Late Ch'ing Times: Chang Chih-tung in Canton, 1884-1889," *Modern Asian Studies*, IV (1970), 325-47.

BEACH, W. "Freedom and Authority in Protestant Ethics" *Journal of Religion*, XXXII (1952), 108-18.

BEAUJON, E. *L'humanisme et la crise de l'autorité.* Lausanne: Editions "Défense de l'Europe," 1950. 85 p.

BELASCO, P. *Authority in Church and State.* London: Allen & Unwin, 1928. 326 p.

BELL, D. R. "Authority" in *The Proper Study: Royal Institute of Philosophy Lectures, 1969-1970.* London: Macmillan, 1971. [pp. 190-203.]

BENDIX, R. *Work and Authority in Industry: Ideologies of Management in the Course of Industrialization.* New York: J. Wiley, 1956. 466 p.

BENN, S. I. "Authority," *The Encyclopedia of Philosophy*, I, 215-218.

BENN, S. I. and R. S. PETERS. *Social Principles and the Democratic State.* London: Allen & Unwin, 1959. 403 p.

BENNE, K. D. *A Conception of Authority: An Introductory Study.* New York: Teachers College, Columbia U., 1943. 227 p. Bibliog: pp. 197-204.

BENNE, K. D. "'Authority in Education," *Harvard Educational Review*,

XL (1970), 385-410.

BENNIS, W. G. "Leadership Theory and Administrative Behavior: The Problem of Authority," *Administrative Science Quarterly,* IV (1959) 259-301.

BENNIS, W. G., N. BERKOWITZ [et al.] "Authority, Power and the Ability to Influence," *Human Relations,* XI (1958), 143-155.

BERDYAEV, N. "Man and Caesar—Authority," in his *The Realm of Spirit and the Realm of Caesar.* Trans. D. A. Lowrie. London: Victor Gollancz Ltd., 1952. [pp. 69-85.]

BERGEVIN, A. de. "Autorité et loi naturelle," *Esprit,* No. 379 (1969), 360-367.

BERLINGER, R. "Signal und Chance: Die Krisis des Autoritätsbewusstseins," *Philosophische Perspektiven,* I (1969), 66-69.

BERNARD, C. "The Theory of Authority" in *Theories of Society,* ed. T. Parsons et al. New York: Free Press, 1961. 2v.

BERTOCCI, P. "The Authority of Ethical Ideals," *Journal of Philosophy,* XXXIII (1936), 269-274.

BIERSTEDT, R. "The Problem of Authority" in Morroe Berger et al. (eds.), *Freedom and Control in Modern Society.* New York: Octagon Books, 1964.

BLAU, P. M. "Critical Remarks on Weber's Theory of Authority," *American Political Science Review,* LVII (1963), 305-16.

BLAU, P. M. "The Hierarchy of Authority in Organizations," *American Journal of Sociology,* LXXIII (1967), 453-467.

BOAS, G. "The Authority of Criticism," Chap. VI of his *A Primer for Critics.* Baltimore: Johns Hopkins, 1937.

BOAS, G. "Parmenides and Authority," *Monist,* XXXI (1921), 224-48.

BOAS, G. "The Rejection of Authority," Chap. 1 of his *Dominant Themes of Modern Philosophy: A History.* New York: The Ronald Press Co., 1957.

BOCHENSKI, J. M. *The Logic of Religion.* New York: N. Y. U. Press, 1965. 179 p. ["Analysis of Authority," pp. 162-173.]

BOCHENSKI, J. M. "On Authority," *Memorias del XII Congreso Internacional de Filosofia.* Mexico: Universidad Nacional Autonoma de Mexico, 1964. [Vol. V, 45-46.]

BOOTH, M. "Freedom and Authority," *Contemporary Review,* CVII (1915), 495-504.

BOŠNJAK, B. "Der Sinn der philosophischen Existenz. Philosophie und Autorität," *Internationale Dialogzeitschrift,* II (1969), 232-41.

BOURRICAUD, F. "Autorité, discussion, contestation," *Cahiers internationaux de sociologie,* XXXI (1961), 81-94.

BOURRICAUD, F. *Esquisse d'une théorie de l'autorité.* Paris: Librairie Plon, 1961. 422 p. [2. ed., 1969.]

BOWE, G. *The Origin of Political Authority.* Dublin: Clonmore & Reynolds, 1955. 102 p.

BRANDIS, R. "On the Noxious Influence of Authority," *Quarterly Review of Economics & Business,* VII (1967), 37-48.

BRANDT, R. "The Use of Authority in Ethics," in his *Ethical Theory.* Englewood Cliffs, N. J.: Prentice-Hall, 1959. [pp. 56-82.]

BRAYBROOKE, D. "Authority as a Subject of Social Science and Philosophy," *Review of Metaphysics,* XIII (1960), 469-85.

BRONSON, W. C., E. S. KATTEN, N. LIVSON. "Patterns of Authority and Affection in Two Generations," *Journal of Abnormal and Social Psychology,* LVIII (1959), 143-152.

BROWN, R. W. "A Determinant of the Relationship between Rigidity and Authoritarianism," *Journal of Abnormal and Social Psychology,* XLVIII (1953), 469-76.

BROWNE, M. "The Source and Purpose of Political Authority," *Studies* (Dublin), XXV (1936), 390-398.

BRYANT, R. H. *The Bible's Authority Today.* Minneapolis: Augsburg Publishing House, 1968. 235 p.

BRYNE, D. "Parental Antecedents of Authoritarianism," *Journal of Personality and Social Psychology,* I (1965), 369-73.

BUDDE, F. *Die Autorität als Erkenntnisquelle.* Bonn: Marcus u. Webers, 1908. 62 p.

BUEHRIG, E. H. "International Pattern of Authority," *World Politics,* XVII (1965), 369-85.

BURKLE, H. R. "The Ground of Biblical Authority," *The Journal of Bible and Religion,* XXV, (1957).

BURRILL, D. R. "Changing Status of Moral Authority," *Harvard Theological Review,* LIX (1966), 241-55.

BURWEN, L. S. and D. T. CAMPBELL. "The Generality of Attitudes towards Authority and Non-authority Figures," *Journal of Abnormal and Social Psychology,* LIV (1957), 24-31.

BUTLER, E. C. *Religions of Authority and the Religion of the Spirit.* London: Sheed & Ward, 1930. 190 p.

BUTLER, J. F. "Authority and Theism," *The Congregational Quarterly,* XIII (1935), 184-93.

BUTTER, W. *Die Autorität des Offiziers.* Berlin: Deutscher Militarverlag, 1966. 130 p.

CAMERON, J. M. *Images of Authority: A Consideration of the Concepts of Regnum and Sacerdotium.* New Haven: Yale U. Press, 1966. 81 p.

CAMPBELL, D. T. "Military Experience and Attitudes Toward Authority," *American Journal of Sociology,* LXII (1957), 482-90.

CANADAY, N. *Melville and Authority.* Gainesville: U. of Florida Press, 1968. 61 p.

CANNING, R. R. and J. M. BARKER. "Effect of the Group on Authoritarian and Non-authoritarian Persons," *American Journal of Sociology,* LXIV (1959), 579-81.

CARROLL, J. D. "Noetic Authority," *Public Administration Review,* XXIX (1969), 492-500.

CASSINELLI, C. W. "Political Authority: Its Exercise and Possession," *Western Political Quarterly,* XIV (1961), 635-646.

CATLIN, G. *A Study of the Principles of Politics, being an Essay Toward Political Rationalization.* New York: The Macmillan Co., 1930. 469 p.

CERTEAU, M. de. "Structures sociales et autorités chrétiennes," *Etudes,* CCCXXIX (1969), 128-42; 285-93.

CHESTERTON, G. K. "Authority or Prejudice," *America,* XLII (1929), 152-153.

CHEVILLE, R. A. *By What Authority? A Series of Lectures Delivered to the Melchisedec Priesthood of Independence, Mo., Jan. 8-13, 1956.* Independence: Herald House, 1956. 96 p.

CHILDS, J. L. "Education and Authority," *Religious Education,* XXXIII (1938), 149-153.

CHRISTIE, R. and P. COOK. "A Guide to Published Literature Relating to the Authoritarian Personality through 1956," *Journal of Psychology,* XLV (1958), 171-99.

CHRISTIE, R. and M. JAHODA (eds.). *Studies in the Scope and Method of "The Authoritarian Personality."* Glencoe, Ill.: The Free Press, 1954. 279 p.

CLARK, B. R. "Faculty Authority," *Bulletin of the American Association of University Professors,* XXVII (1961), 293-302.

COAN, A. L. J. *The Rule of Faith in the Ecclesiastical Writings of the First Two Centuries: An Historico-Apologetical Investigation.* Washington, D. C.: Catholic U. of America, 1924. 116 p. Bibliog: p. 111-116.

COHEN, C. "Autonomy and Government," *Journal of Philosophy,* LXIX (1972), 716.

COKER, F. W. "'Reason of State' and the Doctrine of Political Authority by Force," in *Recent Political Thought,* New York and London: D. Appleton-Century Co., 1934. [pp. 433-59]

COLLIER, K. G. "Authority, Society and Education," *Journal of Educational Sociology,* XXX (1957), 283-288.

COMFORT, A. *Authority and Delinquency in the Modern State: A Crimi-*

nological Approach to the Problem of Power. London: Routledge and K. Paul, 1950. 112 p.

COMMONS, J. R. *A Sociological View of Sovereignty, 1899-1900.* New York: A. M. Kelley, Bookseller, 1965. 109 p.

CONFERENCE ON SCIENCE, PHILOSOPHY AND RELIGION in Their Relation to the Democratic Way of Life. Volume 12: *Freedom and Authority in our Time.* New York: Distributed by Harpers, 1953. 767 p. [Includes articles by D. Bidney, B. Z. Bokser, F. Burke, E. N. Cahn, W. G. Constable, P. Frank, C. Frankel, C. W. Hendel, L. S. Kubie, J. LaFarge, S. P. Lamprecht, G. R. Negley, E. W. Patterson, R. Ulrich, G. Wiegel, and others.]

"CONSCIENCE AND AUTHORITY SYMPOSIUM," *Spritual Life,* XI (1965), 54-92. [Includes articles by C. Henlsey, D. Charlton, T. Margaret, R. Lassance, and E. Hurley.]

COOKE, B. "Who Can Teach Authoritatively?" *Journal of Ecumenical Studies,* VIII (1971), 867-68.

CORBISLEY, T., S. J. and A. MACINTYRE. "Dialogue between Tom and Alisdair: Authority," *Theoria to Theory,* II (1967), 22-28.

COSTER, S. de. "L'exercice de l'autorité, problème de psychologie sociale," *Revue de l'Institut de sociologie* (Bruxelles), XXIV (1951), 35-65.

COULSON, J. "Authority and Radicalism" *Blackfriars,* XLII (1961), 250-61.

CRAGG, G. R. *Reason and Authority in the Eighteenth Century.* Cambridge: University Press, 1964. 349 p.

CRISIS OF AUTHORITY. *The Southern Journal of Philosophy,* VII (1970). 264 p. [Includes articles by A. Kaplan, E. M. Adams, I. Jenkins, and others.]

CROUZEL, H. "Autorité et obéissance: un problème pratique," *Nouvelle Revue Théologique,* LXXXVI (1964), 176-184.

CUNNINGHAM, R. L. "Authority and Morals," *Proceedings of the American Catholic Philosophical Association,* XLIII (1969), 155-164.

CURREN, C. (ed.) *Contraception: Authority and Dissent.* New York: Herder and Herder, 1969. 237 p.

DAHL, R. A. *After the Revolution? Authority in a Good Society.* New Haven: Yale U. P., 1970. 171 p.

DAILLET, J.-M. et P. DE SAINT-ROBERT. "Sur la possibilité d'une autorité mondiale," *Table Ronde,* nos. 234-235 (1967), 29-60.

DALTON, G. W., L. B. BARNES, and A. ZALEZNIK. *The Distribution of Authority in Formal Organizations.* Boston: Harvard University, Division of Research, Graduate School of Business Administration, 1968. 229 p. Bibliog.: pp. 217-223.

DAVID, J. *Loi naturelle et autorité de l'Eglise.* Paris: Editions du Cerf, 1968. 119 p.

DAVIES, R. E. *The Problem of Authority in the Continenetal Reformers: A Study in Luther, Zwingli, and Calvin.* London: The Epworth Press, 1946. 158 p.

DAVIES, R. E. *Religious Authority in an Age of Doubt.* London: The Epworth Press, 1968. 228 p.

DAVIES, W. W. "By What Authority?" *Hibbert Journal,* XXXIV (1935-36), 194-205.

DAY, J. "Authority," *Political Studies,* XI (1963), 257-271.

DE MAETZU, R. *Authority, Liberty and Function.* New York and London: Macmillan, 1916.

DEMOS, R. "On the Decline of Authority," *International Journal of Ethics,* XXXVI (1926), 247-62.

DEPREUX, E. "Crise et mystique de l'autorité," *La Grande Revue,* XXXVIII (1934), 645-48.

DESCAMPS, P. "L'Autorité et la hiérarchie chez les peuples non-civilsés," *Annales de l'Institut international de sociologie,* XV (1928), 85-100.

DEWART, L. "Church and Authority," in his *Religion, Language and Truth,* New York: Herder and Herder, 1970. [pp. 107-25.]

DEWEY, J. "Authority and Resistance to Social Change," in his *Problems of Men,* New York: Philosophical Library, 1946. [pp. 93-110.]

DICKINSON, J. "Social Order and Political Authority," *American Political Science Review,* XXIII (1929), 293-328, 593-632.

DIETZ, H. *Autorität und Ordnung in Schule und Gemeinschaft.* Frankfurt: M. Diesterweg, 1960. 210 p.

DOMINIAN, J. "The Psychological Roots of Authority," *New Blackfriars,* L (1969), 512-23.

DOUGLAS, J. E. "Principle of Authority," *Thought,* XIV (1939), 185-8.

DOWD, J. *Control in Human Societies.* New York, London: D. Appleton-Century Company, Inc., 1936. 475 p. Bibliog.: pp. 437-441; 451-475.

DRANE, J. *Authority and Institutions: A Study in Church Crisis.* Milwaukee: Bruce, 1969. 193 p.

DRESSEN, W. (ed.) *Antiautoritäres Lager und Anarchismus.* Berlin: Wagenback, 1968. 157 p.

DUCONSEIL, M. *Machiavel et Montesquieu, recherche sur un principe d'autorité.* Paris: Denoël, 1943. 279 p.

DUESBERG, H. "La soumission aux autorités" *Bible et vie Chrétienne,* No. 73 (1967), 15-26.

DUHAMEL, G. "Sens de l'autorité," *Mercure de France,* CCLXIX (1936),

449-52.

DUNAN, C. "Autorité et liberté," *Revue Philosophique*, LIX (1905), 147-179.

DU PRINCIPE DE L'AUTORITÉ DEPUIS 1789, SUIVI DE NOUVELLES CONSIDÉRATIONS SUR LE MÊME SUJET. Paris: Plon Frères, 1853, 71 p.

DUROC, P. "Liberté et autorité," *Civilisation nouvelle*, I (1938), 148-161.

DWORKIN, G. "Reasons and Authority," *Journal of Philosophy*, LXIX (1972), 716-18.

EBENSTEIN, W. (ed.) *Great Political Thinkers*. New York: Holt, Rinehart and Winston, 1960. 978 p. [Includes articles by M. Luther, Marsilius of Padua, J. S. Mill, and A. de Tocqueville.]

EDGERTON, S. G. "Have We Really Talked Enough About 'Authority'?" *Studies in Philosophy and Education*, VI (1969), 369-83.

EDINGER, L. J. *Political Leadership in Industrialized Societies: Studies in Comparative Analysis*. New York: Wiley, 1967. 376 p. Bibliog.: pp. 348-366.

EGERTON, H. "The Nature of Political Authority," *Oxford and Cambridge Review*, No. 19 (1912), 123-36.

ENGEL, S. *Equality and Authority: A Study of Class Status and Power in Australia*. London: Tavistock, 1970. 492 p.

ENGELS, F. "On Authority" in K. Marx and F. Engels, *Selected Works*, Moscow: FLPH, 1958, 2 v. [Vol. I, p. 636-39.]

ESCHENBURG, T. *Über Autorität*. Frankfurt a.M.: Suhrkamp, 1965. 181 p. Bibliog.: pp. 179-182.

ESLICK, L. J. "The Republic Revisited: The Dilemma of Liberty and Authority," *Philosophy Forum*, X (1971), 171-212.

FALK, R. A. *The Authority of the United Nations over Non-members*. Princeton: Center of International Studies, Woodrow Wilson School of Public and International Affairs, Princeton U., 1965. 101 p.

FALLER, F. *Die rechtsphilosophische Begründung der gesellschaftlichen und staatlichen Autorität bei Thomas von Aquin. Eine problemgeschichtliche Untersuchung*. Heidelberg: F. H. Kerle, 1954. 86 p.

FESSARD, G. *Autorité et bien commun*. 2. ed. Paris: Aubier-Montaigne, 1969. 145 p.

FIELD, O. P. "Property and Authority: The Modification of Property Rights Under American Law," *Journal of Politics*, III (1941), 253-75.

FOLZ, R. "Sur le principe de l'autorité au moyen âge," *Revue des sciences religieuses*, XXXVII (1963), 27-33.

FORSYTH, P. T. *The Principle of Authority in Relation to Certainty,*

Sanctity and Society: An Essay in the Philosophy of Experimental Religion. 2d ed. London: Independent Press, 1952. 430 p.

FOX, R. M. "Two Kinds of Authority," *Philosophy in Context*, I (1972), 32-35.

FRANKEL, C. "Political Disobedience and the Denial of Political Authority," *Social Theory and Practice*, II (1972), 85-98.

FREEDMAN, M., H. WEBSTER and N. SANFORD. "A Study of Authoritarianism and Psychopathology," *Journal of Psychology*, XLI (1965), 315-22.

FREIDSON, E. "The Imparity of Professional Authority," *Institutions and the Person*, H. Becker et al. (eds.), Chicago: Aldine Pub. Co., 1968. [pp. 25-34]

FRIEDMAN, R. B. "An Introduction to Mill's Theory of Authority," in J. B. Schneewind (ed.). *Mill: A Collection of Critical Essays,* Notre Dame: U. of Notre Dame Press, 1969. [pp. 397-425.]

FRIEDMANN, F. G. "Jugend und Autorität," *Pedagogische Weit*, XXXIII (1969), 60-62.

FRIEDRICH, C. J. (ed.) *Nomos I: Authority.* Cambridge Mass.: Harvard U. P., 1958. 234 p. [Includes articles by C. W. Hendel, C. J. Friedrich, H. J. Spiro, J. Hall, F. H. Knight, H. Arendt, G. E. C. Catlin, N. Jacobson, W. H. Kraus, B. de Jouvenal, D. Easton, T. Parsons, and E. A. Hoebel.]

FRIEDRICH, C. J. *Man and His Government.* New York: McGraw Hill, 1963. 737 p. [Chap. 12: "Political Authority and Reasoning."]

FRIEDRICH, C. J. "Power and Authority" in his *An Introduction to Political Theory,* New York: Harper and Row, 1967. [pp. 121-32.]

FRIEDRICH, C. J. *Tradition and Authority.* London: Macmillan, 1972. 144 p.

FROST, S. B. *Die Autoritätslehre in den Werken John Wesleys.* München: E. Reinhardt, 1938. 110 p.

FULLERTON, K. *Prophecy and Authority.* New York: Macmillan, 1919. 214 p.

GAMMON, F. L. "The Philosophical Thought of Yves Simon: A Brief Survey," *Revue de l'Université d'Ottawa*, XLII (1972), 237-44.

GARDNER, N. D. *The Act of Delegating.* Garden City, N. Y.: Doubleday, 1965. 126 p.

GEISSLER, E. E. (ed.) *Autorität und Erziehung.* Bad Heilbrunn/Obb.: Klinkhardt, 1965. 135 p.

GELDONHUYS, J. N. *Supreme Authority: The Authority of the Lord, His Apostles and the New Testament.* Grand Rapids: Eerdmans, 1953. 128 p.

GERSON, W. "Autorität und Respect heute," *Unsere Jugend,* XXI (1969), 193-206.

GIBBONS, B. W. "Problem of Authority: Reply with Editorial Comment," *America,* CVII, (1962), 1016, 1028-29.

GIERKE, O. VON. *Poliitcal Theories of the Middle Ages.* Trans. by F. W. Maitland. Cambridge: University Press, 1900. 197 p.

GINI, C. "Authority and the Individual during the Different Stages of the Evolution of Nations," *Scientia* LXVI (1937), 177-185, 295-306.

GLADSTONE, W. E. *Gleanings of Past Years, 1843-78.* New York: Charles Scribner's Sons, 1879. [See Vol. 3.]

GODFREY, F. LaT. "The Idea of Authority," *Hermathena,* XCI (1958), 3-19.

GOGARTEN, F. *Wider die Achtung der Autorität.* Jena: E. Diederichs, 1930. 45 p.

GOLIGHTLY, C. L. "Ethics and Moral Activism," *Monist,* LVI (1972), 576-86.

GOULDNER, A. W. (ed.) *Studies in Leadership.* New York: Russell & Russell, 1965. 736 p. [Includes articles related to authority by J. F. Wolpert, D. Bell, and K. Lewin.]

GRANADO, C. "Autoridad y vida religiosa," *Manresa,* XL (1968), 207.

GRAY, C. *Filosofia del diritto e filosofia dell' autorità.* Milano: Sodalitas, 1938. 91 p.

GRAZIA, S. de. "Authority and Rationality," *Philosophy,* XXVII (1952), 99-109.

GRAZIA, S. de. "The Principle of Authority in Its Relation to Freedom," *Educational Forum,* XV (1951), 145-55.

GRAZIA, S. de. "What Authority Is Not," *American Political Science Review,* LIII (1959), 321-331.

GREEN, G. "The Question of Authority," in *The New Radicalism: Anarchist or Marxist?,* New York: International Publishers, 1971. [pp. 31-34.]

GREENSTEIN, F. "The Benevolent Leader: Children's Images of Political Authority," *American Political Science Review,* LIV (1900), 934-943.

GREENSTEIN, F. "Personality and Political Socialization: The Theories of Authoritarian and Democratic Character," *Annals of the American Academy of Political and Social Science,* CCCLXI (1965), 81-95.

GREGORY, W. E. "The Orthodoxy of the Authoritarian Personality," *Journal of Social Psychology,* XLV (1957), 217-32.

GRUNDSTEIN, N. D. *Presidential Delegation of Authority in Wartime.* Pittsburgh: U. of Pittsburgh Press, 1961. 106 p.

GRUSKY, O. "Authoritarianism and Effective Indoctrination: A Case Study," *Administrative Science Quarterly,* VII (1962), 79-95.

GUARDINI, R. *Power and Responsibility: A Course of Action for the New Age.* Trans. by E. C. Briefs. Chicago: Regnery, 1961. 104 p.

GUINAN, M. A. *Freedom and Authority in Education.* Washington, D. C.: Catholic University, 1936. 117 p.

HALL, F. J. *Authority, Eccelesiastical and Biblical.* New York: Longmans, Green and Co., 1908. 300 p.

HALLOWELL, J. H. *The Moral Foundation of Democracy.* Chicago, U. of Chicago Press, 1954. 134 p.

HAMPE, J. C. (ed.) *Die Autorität der Freiheit Gegenwart des Konzils und Zukunft der Kirche im ökumenischen Disput.* München: Kösel, 1967. 3v.

HANDCOCK, W. D. "The Function and Nature of Authority in Society," *Philosophy,* XXVIII (1953), 99-112.

HANDLIN, O. and M. (eds.) *The Popular Sources of Political Authority: Documents on the Massachusetts Constitution of 1780.* Cambridge, Mass.: Harvard U. Press, 1966. 962 p.

HARRIS, E. "Sovereign Authority and Power" (Chap III) in his *Annihilation and Utopia: The Principles of International Politics.* London: George Allen & Unwin Ltd., 1966. 331 p.

HARRISON, P. *Authority and Power in the Free Church Tradition: A Social Case Study of the American Baptist Convention.* Princeton: Princeton U. Press, 1959. 248 p.

HARRISON, P. "Weber's Categories of Authority and Voluntary Associations," *American Sociological Review,* XXV (1960), 232-7. [Reply with rejoinder, J. G. Butler, XXV (1960), 731-2.]

HART, H. L. A. *The Concept of Law.* Oxford: Clarendon Press, 1961. 263 p.

HARTFIEL, G. (ed.) *Die autoritäre Gesellschaft.* Köln: Westdeutscher Verlag, 1969. 215 p.

HARTMANN, H. *Authority and Organization in German Management.* Princeton: Princeton U. Press, 1959. 318 p. Bibliog.: pp. 297-309.

HARTMANN, H. *Funktionale Autorität; systematische Abhandlung zu einem soziologischen Begriff.* Stuttgart: F. Enke, 1964. 143 p.

HARVARD TERCENTENARY CONFERENCE OF ARTS AND SCIENCES, 1936. *Authority and the Individual.* Cambridge, Mass.: Harvard U. Press, 1937. 371 p. [Includes articles by J. Dewey, W. Jaeger, W. C. Mitchell, and others.]

HAWKINS, E. *The Duty of Private Judgment: A Sermon Preached Be-*

fore the University of Oxford, Nov. 11, 1838. Oxford: J. H. Parker, 1838. 34 p.

HAY, D. "Authority and Democracy," New Blackfriars L (1969), 323-27.

HEGEL, G. W. F. "Authority and Freedom," in Q. Lauer, Hegel's Idea of Philosophy, New York: Fordham U. Press, 1971. [pp. 148-59.]

HEIMLER, E. (ed.) Resistance Against Tyranny: A Symposium. London: Routledge & K. Paul, 1966. 168 p.

HEINTZ, P. Die Autoritätsproblematik bei Proudhon; Versuch einer immanenten Kritik. Köln: Verlag für Politik und Wirtschaft, 1956. 222 p. Bibliog.: pp. 220-222.

HEINZE, R. "Auctoritas," Hermes, IX (1925), 348-66.

HENDEL, C. W. "The Meaning of Obligation," in Barrett, C. L. (ed.) Contemporary Idealism in America, New York: Russell & Russell, 1964. [pp. 239-95.]

HESS, R. D. "The Socialization of Attitudes Toward Political Authority: Some Cross-national Comparisons," International Social Science Journal, XV (1963), 542-559.

HEUSS, J. "The Advantage of Authority in Religious Education," Religious Education, XXXIII (1938), 154-157.

HIPPEL, E. Gewaltenteilung im modernen Staate. Köln: Verlag Deutsche Glocke, 1950. 59 p.

HITCHCOCK, J. "The State of Authority in the Church," Cross Currents, XX (1970), 369-381.

HODGKINSON, H. L. and L. R. MEETH (eds.) Power and Authority: Transformation of Campus Governance. San Francisco: Jossey-Bass, 1971. 208 p.

HODGSON, L. "Authority," in Essays in Christian Philosophy, London, New York: Longmans, Green and Co., 1930. [pp. 116-27.]

HOFFMAN, R. J. S. "Authority and Tyranny," American Review, IV (1935), 385-409.

HOFFMAN, R. J. S. "Liberty and Authority," American Review, III (1934), 562-90.

HOLLISTER, W. W. Government and the Arts of Obedience. New York: King's Crown Press, 1948. 139 p. Bibliog.: pp. 131-134.

HOPKINS, T. K. "Bureaucratic Authority: The Convergence of Weber and Barnard," in Amitai Etzioni (ed.) Complex Organizations. New York: Holt, Rinehart, and Winston, 1961. [pp. 82-100.]

HORST, J. J. "Authority in Scholastic Philosophy," Ecclesiastical Review, CIV (1941), 244-51.

HUBERT, R. Le principe d'autorité dans l'organisation démocratique. Paris:

Gamber, 1926. 224 p.

HUIZINGA, A. *The Authority of Might and Right.* Boston: Sherman, French & Co., 1911. 40 p.

HUNKIN, J. W. "Vision and Authority," *Modern Churchman,* XIX (1929), 501-4.

HUNTINGTON, S. P. and C. H. MOORE (eds.) *Authoritarian Politics in Modern Society: The Dynamics of Established One-party Systems.* New York: Basic Books, 1970. 533 p.

ILLINGWORTH, J. R. *Divine Transcendence and its Reflection in Religious Authority.* London: Macmillan and Co., Ltd., 1911. 255 p.

INSTITUTE OF SOCIAL RESEARCH, New York. *Authority and the Family.* New York, 1937. 174 p. [A partial translation of *Studien über autorität und Familie.* Paris: F. Alcan, 1936. 947 p.]

IVERACH, J. "Authority" in James Hastings, *Encyclopedia of Religion and Ethics,* New York: C. Scribner's Sons, 1951. [Vol. II, pp. 249-54.]

JACKSON, F. "A Note on Incorrigibility and Authority," *Australasian Journal of Philosophy,* XLV (1967), 358-63.

JANOWITZ, M. "Changing Patterns of Organizational Authority: the Military Establishment," *Administrative Science Quarterly,* III (1959), 473-93.

JANOWITZ, M. and D. MARVICK. "Authoritarianism and Political Behavior," *Public Opinion Quarterly,* XVII (1953), 185-201.

JANSSENS, L. *Droits personnels et autorité.* Louvain: Editions Nauwelaerts, 1954. 77 p.

JASPERS, K. *The Idea of a University.* Trans. by H. A. T. Reiche and H. F. Vanderschmidt. Boston: Beacon Press, 1959. 135 p.

JASPERS, K. "Liberty and Authority," in his *Philosophy and the World.* Trans. by E. B. Ashton. Chicago: Regnery, 1963. [pp. 33-56.]

JENSEN, A. R. "Authoritarian Attitudes and Personality Maladjustment," *Journal of Abnormal and Social Psychology,* LIV (1957), 303-311.

JERROLD, D. "Authority, Mind and Power," *The Criterion,* XII (1932-33), 223-43.

JOHNSON, C. "The Changing Nature and Locus of Authority in Communist China," in J. Lindbeck (ed.), *China: Management of a Revolutionary Society,* Seattle: U. of Washington Press, 1971. [pp. 34-76.]

JOHNSON, R. C. *Authority in Protestant Theology.* Philadelphia: Westminster Press, 1959. 224 p.

JOOS, H. F. und F. POGGELLER. *Moderne Jugend und neue Autorität.* Freiberg, Basel, Wien: Herder, 1965. 79 p.

JOUSTEN, A. "Autorité et obéissance," *Revue ecclésiastique de Liège*, LII (1966), 321-338.

JOUVENAL, B. de. *On Power, Its Nature and the History of Its Growth.* Tr. by J. F. Huntington. New York: Viking Press, 1949. 421 p.

JOUVENAL, B. de. *Pure Theory of Politics.* Cambridge: University Press, 1963. 220 p.

JOUVENAL, B. de. *Sovereignty: An Inquiry into the Political Good.* Trans. by J. F. Huntington. Chicago: U. of Chicago Press, 1957. 319 p.

KAFTAN, J. "Authority as a Principle of Theology," *American Journal of Theology*, IV (1900), 673-733.

KARIEL, H. S. *In Search of Authority: Twentieth-Century Political Thought.* New York: Free Press, 1964. 258 p.

KEETON, M. *Shared Authority on Campus.* Washington, D.C.: American Association for Higher Education, 1971. 168 p.

KENNY, J. P. "Oases of the International Military Tribunal's Authority," *Thomist*, XI (1948), 197-217.

KERNAN, F. "The Peregrinations of Authority," *The Catholic World*, CXL (1934), 59-67.

KERSCHENSTEINER, G. *Autorität und Freiheit als Bildungsgrundsätze.* 4. Aufl. Leipzig: G. Martin Verlag, 1927. 140 p.

KIERKEGAARD, S. *On Authority and Revelation.* Princeton: Princeton U. Press, 1955. 205 p.

KIM, Y. C. "Authority: Some Conceptual and Empirical Notes," *Western Political Quarterly*, XIX (1966), 223-34.

KIMPEL, B. F. *Faith and Moral Authority.* New York: Philosophical Library, 1953. 186 p.

KIRSCHT, J. P. *Dimensions of Authoritarianism: A Review of Research and Theory* by John P. Kirscht and Ronald C. Dillehay. Lexington: U. of Kentucky Press, 1967. 168 p. Bibliog.: pp. 137-159.

KNOPFELMACHER, F. and D. ARMSTRONG. "Authoritarianism, Ethnocentrism and Religious Denomination," *American Catholic Sociological Review*, XXIV (1963), 99-114.

KNUTSSON, K. E. *Authority and Change: A Study of the Kallu Institution Among the Macha Galla of Ethiopia.* Göteborg, 1967. 239 p.

KREITZER, D. J. "Problems of the Origin of Political Authority," *Philosophical Studies*, X (1960), 190-203.

KREMS, G. und R. MUMM [eds.] *Autorität in der Krise.* Regensburg: Pustet, 1970. 175 p.

KREŠIĆ, A. "Politischer absolutismus, anarchie und autorität," *Praxis*, III (1967), 188-200.

KROPOTKIN, P. *Law and Authority*. London: International Publishing Co., 1886. 23 p.

KRUYTBOSCH, C. E. and S. L. MESSINGER. "State of the University: Authority and Change," *The American Behavioral Scientist*, XI (1968), 1-48.

KUNZE, J. *Glaubensregel, Heilige Schift und Taufbekenntnis. Untersuchungen über die dogmatische Autorität, Ihr Werden und ihre Geschichte, vornehnilich in der alten Kirche*. Leipzig: Dörffling & Franke, 1899. 560 p.

LABERTHONNIÈRE, L. *The Ideal Teacher or the Catholic Notion of Authority in Education*. Tr. by M. LaForge. New York: Cathedral Library Association, 1902. 81 p.

LABERTHONNIÈRE, L. *Théorie de l'éducation*. 10. éd. Paris: Vrin, 1935. [Chap. III "L'autorité éducatrice".]

LA BRIÈRE, Y. de. *Comment concilier autorité et liberté?* Paris: E. Flammarion, 1929. 120 p.

LADENSON, R. F. "Legitimate Authority," *American Philosophical Quarterly*, IX (1972), 335-41.

LADENSON, R. F. "Wolff on Legitimate Authority," *Philosophical Studies*, XXIII (1972), 376-84.

LAIRD, D. A. and E. C. LAIRD. *The Techniques of Delegating: How to Get Things Done Through Others*. New York: McGraw Hill, 1957. 195 p.

LAIRD, J. "The Conception of Authority," *Proceedings of the Aristotelian Society*. N. S. XXXIV (1934), 87-100.

LALLEY, J. M. *Faith and Force: An Inquiry into the Nature of Authority*. Washington, 1946. 19 p. [Human Events Pamphlet, No. 4.]

LANE, R. *The Discovery of Freedom: Man's Struggle Against Authority*. New York: The John Day Co., 1943. 262 p.

LAPLANTE, R. "L'autorité dans la famille," *Culture*, XXVIII (1967), 159-166.

LARIVIÈRE, F. "L'autorité et le changement social dans la relation jeunes-adultes," *Prospectives*, III (1967), 260-266.

LASKI, H. J. *Authority in the Modern State*. New Haven: Yale U. Press, 1919. 398 p.

LASWELL, H. D. and A. KAPLAN. *Power and Society*, New Haven: Yale U. Press, 1950. 294 p.

LAUER, Q. "Authority in the Contemporary World," *Thought*, XLV (1970), 325-45.

LAVALETTE, H. de. "Aperçus sur l'autorité de l'église et l'autorité dans l'église," *Etudes*, CCCXXX (1969), 59-67.

LAVERGNE, B. *Individualisme contre autoritarisme; trois siècles de conflits expliqués par le dualisme social.* Paris: Presses Universitaires de France, 1959. 126 p.

LAVERY, B. "Authority in the Church," *Studies, An Irish Quarterly of Letters, Philosophy, and Science,* LVI (1967), 376-381.

LEAVITT, H. J., H. HAX and J .H. ROCHE. " 'Authoritarianism' and Agreement with Things Authoritative," *Journal of Psychology,* XL (1955), 215-21.

LECKIE, J. *Authority in Religion.* Edinburgh: T. & T. Clark, 1909. 238 p.

LEDER, L. H. *Liberty and Authority: Early American Political Ideology, 1689-1763.* Chicago: Quadrangle Books, 1968. 167 p.

LE FEVRE, L. *Liberty and Restraint.* New York: A. A. Knopf, 1931. 346 p. Bibliog.: pp. 337-346.

LEITES, N. C. and C. WOLF. *Rebellion and Authority: An Analytic Essay on Insurgent Conflicts.* Chicago: Markham Pub. Co., 1970. 174 p.

LEVENTHAL, H., R. JACOBS and H. KUDIRKA. "Authoritarianism, Ideology, and Political Candidate Choice," *Journal of Abnormal and Social Psychology,* LXIX (1964), 539-49.

LEVI, A. W. *Humanism and Politics: Studies in the Relationship of Power and Value in the Western Tradition.* Bloomington: Indiana U. Press, 1969. 508 p.

LEVINSON, D. J. "Authoritarian Personality and Foreign Policy," *Journal of Conflict Resolution,* I (1957), 37-47.

LEWIS, SIR G. C. *An Essay on the Influence of Authority in Matters of Opinion,* 2d ed. London: Longmans, Green and Co., 1875, 260 p.

LICHTENSTEIN, E. *Erziehung, Autorität, Verantwortung. Reflexionen zu einer pädagogischen Ethik.* Ratingen: Henn, 1967. 87 p.

LIPSET, S. M. "Democracy and Working Class Authoritarianism," *American Sociological Review,* XXIV (1959), 482-501.

LIPSITZ, L. "Working Class Authoritarianism: A Re-evaluation," *American Sociological Review,* XXX (1965), 103-109.

LIPSON, L. "Sources of Authority," in his *Great Issues of Politics,* Englewood Cliffs, N. J.: Prentice-Hall, 1954. [pp. 214-38.]

LITTLE, R. D. "Legislative Authority in the Soviet Political System," *Slavic Review,* XXX (1971), 57-73.

LLOYD-JONES, D. M. *Authority.* Chicago: Inter-varsity Press, 1958. 94 p.

LOBANOW-ROSTOVSKY, A. "The Problem of Authority," *Hibbert Journal,* XXV (1926-27), 577-82.

LUCA, F. de. "Le principe de l'autorité dans les états modernes," *Annales de l'Institut international de sociologie,* XV (1928), 149-59.

LUEBKE, N. R. "Hegel's Image and His Views on Social Authority,"

Southwestern Journal of Philosophy, II (1971), 139-51.

LÜTCKE, K. *"Auctoritas" bei Augustin, mit einer Einleitung zur römischen Vorgeschichte des Begriffs.* Stuttgart: W. Kohlhammer, 1968. 223 p.

LUTHER, M. "On Civil Authority," *Open Court,* XXXI (1917), 478-95.

LUTHER, M. *Secular Authority: To What Extent It Should be Obeyed,* in *Works of Martin Luther.* Philadelphia: Muhlenberg Press, 1930. [Vol. III, 223-73.]

LYNMAN, G. J. *The Good Political Ruler According to St. Thomas Aquinas.* Washington: Catholic U. of America Press, 1953. 42 p. Bibliog.: pp. 37-42.

MC CONNELL, F. J. *Christianity and Coercion.* Nashville: Cokesbury Press, 1933. 128 p.

MC COY, C. N. R. "Note on the Problem of the Origin of Political Authority," *Thomist,* XVI (1953), 71-81.

MACDONALD, A. J. M. *Authority and Reason in the Early Middle Ages.* London: Oxford U. Press, 1933. 136 p.

MC KENZIE, J. *Authority in the Church.* New York: Sheed and Ward, 1966. 184 p.

MACKEY, J. P. (ed.) *Morals, Law and Authority: Sources and Attitudes in the Church.* Dayton: Pflaum Press, 1969. 154 p.

MACKINNON, D. M. "Autorité et conscience," in *L'Emeneutica della Libertà Religiosa,* Padova: Cedam, 1968. [pp. 425-430.]

MC NABB, V. J. *Infallibility.* London: Sheed and Ward, 1927. 93 p.

MC PHERSON, T. *Political Obligation.* London: Routledge & Kegan Paul; New York: Humanities Press, 1967. 86 p.

MÄRKER, F. *Autokraten und Demokraten; charakterologische Bildnisse.* Erlenbach-Zürich: E. Rentsch, 1930. 117 p.

MAEZTU, R. *Authority, Liberty and Function in the Light of the War: A Critque of Authority and Liberty as the Foundations of the Modern State and an Attempt to Base Societies on the Principle of Function.* London: G. Allen & Unwin Ltd.; New York: The Macmillan Co., 1916. 288 p.

MAGDELAIN, A. *Auctoritas principis.* Paris: Société d'Edition "Les Belles Lettres," 1947. 120 p. Bibliog.: pp. 117-120.

MAHER, J. "Conscience and Legitimate Authority: Reply to G. Zahn with Rejoinder," *Commonweal,* LXXVI (1962), 151-2.

MAJOR, H. D. A. "Scriptural Authority and Ecclesiastical Authority," *Modern Churchman,* XXXII (1942), 547-52.

MANCEL de BACILLY, P. *Du Pouvoir et de la liberté.* 2. ed. Paris: Dentu, 1853. 301 p.

MANSCHRECK, C. L. (ed.) *Erosion of Authority.* Nashville: Abingdon Press, 1971. 128 p. Bibliog.: pp. 123-125.

MARCUSE, H. "A Study on Authority," in his *Studies in Critical Philosophy*, London: NLB, 1972. [pp. 49-155.]

MARITAIN, J. "Democracy and Authority," in his *Scholaticism and Politics*, New York: The Macmillan Co., 1940. [pp. 89-117.]

MARSAL, M. *L'autorité.* Paris: Presses Universitaires de France, 1958. 124 p.

MARSHALL, T. H. "Authority and the Family," *Sociological Review*, XXIX (1937), 1-19.

MARSTON, G. W. *The Voice of Authority.* Nutley, N. J.: Presbyterian and Reformed Pub. Co., 1960. 110 p.

MARTINEAU, J. *The Seat of Authority in Religion.* 5th ed. London: Lindsey Press, 1905. 733 p.

MEAD, M. *Soviet Attitudes Toward Authority: An Interdisciplinary Approach to Problems of Soviet Character.* New York: McGraw Hill, 1951. 148 p.

MEISSNER, W. W. *The Assault on Authority: Dialogue or Dilemma?* Maryknoll, N.Y.: Orbis Books, 1971. 320 p.

MENNE, A. "Zur formalen structur der autorität," *Kantstudien*, LX (1969), 289-297.

MERRIAM, C. E. *Political Power, its Composition and Incidence.* New York and London: Whittlesey House, McGraw Hill Book Co., Inc., 1934. 331 p.

MESSINEO, A. *Autorità e libertà.* Rome: Raggio, 1946. 24 p. [Also in *Civiltà Cattolica*, n. 2271 (1945).]

MESSINEO, A. "Popolo e autorità," *Civiltà Cattolica*, n. 2265 (1944).

METZ, H. W. and C. A. H. THOMSON. *Authoritarianism and the Individual.* Washington: Brookings Institute, 1950. 371 p.

MICHEL-LÉVY, J. "Problème de l'autorité," *La Grande Revue*, XXXVII (1933), 588-96.

MIGNOT, HENRI. *L'Autorité libératrice.* Paris: Edit. soc. française, 1947. 236 p.

MILFORD, T. R. "Gradations of Authority," *Theology*, CX (1957), 359-365.

MILL, J. S. "Limits of Authority: A Liberal View: Excerpt from 'On Liberty'," in Utley, T. E. and J. S. MacLure, eds. *Documents of Modern Political Thought*, Cambridge: University Press, 1957. [pp. 36-45.]

MILLER, W. B. "Two Concepts of Authority," *American Anthropologist*, N. S. LVII (1955), 271-289.

MÖBUS, G. *Autorität und Disziplin in der Demokratie.* Köln: Westdeutscher Verlag, 1959. 35 p.

MONOD, L. *Le problème de l'autorité.* 3. ed. Paris: Fischbacher, 1923. 213 p.

MONTAGUE, W. P. "The Method of Authoritarianism." Chap. I of his *The Ways of Knowing.* New York: Macmillan, 1925.

MORICK, H. "Is Ultimate Epistemic Authority a Distinguishing Characteristic of the Psychological?" *American Philosophical Quarterly,* VIII (1971), 292-95.

MOURAVIEFF, B. *Le problème de l'autorité super-étatique.* Neuchâtel: La Baconnière, 1950. 132 p. Bibliog.: pp. 125-126.

MOUZON, E. *Preaching with Authority.* Garden City, N. Y.: Doubleday, Doran & Co., Inc., 1929. 245 p.

MURPHY, A. E. "An Ambiguity in Professor Simon's Philosophy of Democratic Government," *Philosophical Review,* LXI (1952), 198-211.

MURRAY, R. H. "Conscience and Authority," *Contemporary Review,* CXXXV (1929), 56-63.

NASH, P. *Authority and Freedom in Education.* New York: Wiley, 1966, 342 p.

NEGLEY, G. R. *Political Authority and Moral Judgment.* Durham, N. C.: Duke U. Press, 1965, 163 p.

NEHEMKIS, R. R. "Public Authority: Some Legal and Practical Aspects," *Yale Law Journal,* XLVII (1938), 14-33.

NELIS, H. J. *Die Autorität als pädagogisches Problem.* Kalmüng: M. Lassleben, 1933. 301 p.

NEWMAN, H. *An Essay in Aid of a Grammar of Assent.* Garden City, N. Y.: Image Books, 1955. 396 p.

NISBET, R. "The Nemesis of Authority," *Encounter,* XXXIX (1972), 11-21. [Also in *Intercollegiate Review,* VIII (1972), 3-13.]

OAKESHOTT, M. "Authority of the State," *Modern Churchman,* XIX (1929), 313-27.

OGILVY, J. A. "Socratic Method, Platonic Method and Authority," *Educational Theory,* XXI (1971), 3-16.

OMAN, J. *Vision and Authority.* London: Hodder and Stoughton, 1902. 344 p.

O'MEARA, T. F. and C. S. CALIAN. "Is There a Common Authority for Christians?" *Ecumenical Review,* XXII (1970), 16-35.

ORR, R. R. *Reason and Authority: The Thought of William Chillingworth.* London: Oxford U. Press, 1967. 217 p.

OTTEN, C. M. *University Authority and the Student: The Berkeley Experience.* Berkeley: U. of California Press, 1970. 222 p.

OTTENBERG, S. *Leadership and Authority in an African Society: The*

Afikpo-Village Group. Seattle: U. of Washington Press, 1972. 324 p.

PALMÈS, F. M. *¿Como educar? Autoridad y disciplina.* 2. ed. corr. y aumentada. Barcelon: Institute Filosófico de Balmesiana, 1956. 125 p.

PARKER, D. H. "Rhetoric, Ethics and Manipulation," *Philosophy and Rhetoric,* V (1972), 69-87.

PARSONS, E. W. *Social Rule: A Study of the Will to Power.* New York and London: G. P. Putnam's Sons, 1916. 185 p.

PATRICK, M. J. "Supreme Court and Authority Acceptance," *Western Political Quarterly,* XXI (1968), 5-19.

PAUTRAT, B. "Du sujet politique et des ses intérêts: note sur la théorie humienne de l'autorité," *Cahiers pour l'Analyse,* II (1967), 67-74

PEABODY, R. L. *Organizational Authority: Superior-Subordinate Relationships in Three Public Service Organizations.* New York: Atherton Press, 1964. 163 p.

PEABODY, R. L. "Perceptions of Organizational Authority: A Comparative Analysis," *Administrative Science Quarterly,* VI (1962), 463-482.

PECK, G. *Appeal from Tradition to Scripture and Common Sense; or An Answer to the Question, What Constitutes the Divine Rule of Faith and Practice.* New York: G. Lane, 1844. 472 p.

PEIRCE, C. S. "Fixation of Belief" in his *Chance, Love and Logic,* ed. M. R. Cohen. New York: G. Braziller, 1956. 318 p.

PERELMAN, C. "Autorité, Idéologie et Violence," in his *Le Champ de l'Argumentation,* Bruxelles: Presses Universitaires de Bruxelles, 1970.

PERKINS, L. H. "On Reconciling Autonomy and Authority," *Ethics,* LXXXII (1972), 114-23.

PETERS, R. S. "Authority," in A. De Crespigny and A. Wertheimer (eds.), *Contemporary Political Theory,* New York: Atherton, 1970. [pp. 60-73.]

PETERS, R. S. *Authority, Responsibility, and Education,* New York: Atherton, 1965. 137 p.

PETERS, R. S. "The Nature of Authority," *Listener,* LXI (1959), 243-4.

PETRIE, C. "Revival of Authority and its Intellectual Background," *19th Century,* CVIII (1928), 613-23.

PIACENTINI, T. *Introduzione alla "Filosofia dell' autorità" di G. B. Vico.* Rome: Ip. Failli, 1947. 200 p.

PIPPING, K. *Gespräche mit der deutschen Jugend; ein Beitrag zum Autoritätsproblem,* von Knut Pipping, Rudolf Abshagen und Anne-Eva Braunek. Helsingfors, 1954. 437 p.

PISIER, E. *Autorité et liberté dans les écrits politiques de Bertrand de Jouvenal.* Paris: Presses Universitaires de France, 1967. 92 p.

PLAMENATZ, J. *Man and Society: Political and Social Theory.* New York:

McGraw Hill, 1963. 2v.

POLANYI, M. "Authority and Conscience," in his *Science, Faith and Society*, Chicago: Chicago U. Press, 1969. 96 p. [pp. 42-62.]

POUND, R. "Authority and the Individual Reason," *Harvard Divinity School Bulletin*, XLI (1944), n. 21.

POUND, R. "Idea of Authority," in Catholic U. of America, School of Law, *Jubilee Law Lectures. 1889-1939*. Washington, D. C.: Catholic U. of America Press, 1939. [pp. 26-46.]

LE POUVOIR. (Annales de Philosophie Politique 1 & 2.) Paris: Presses Universitaires, 1956-1957. 2v. [Articles by R. McKeon, J. Maritain and others.]

PRANGER, R. J. "An Explanation for Why Final Political Authority is Necessary," *American Political Science Review*, LX (1966), 994-998.

PRESTHUS, R. V. "Authority in Organizations" *Public Administration Review*, XX (1960), 86-91.

PROCEEDINGS OF THE ARISTOTELIAN SOCIETY. "Symposium: Authority," Suppl. Vol. 32 (1958) [Articles by R. S. Peters, P. Winch, and A. Duncan-Jones.]

PYE, L. W. *The Authority Crisis in Chinese Politics*. Chicago: U. of Chicago, Center for Policy Study, 1967. 35 p.

PYE, L. W. *The Spirit of Chinese Politics: A Psychocultural Study of the Authority Crisis in Political Development*. Cambridge, Mass.: M. I. T. Press, 1968. 255 p.

QUINTON, A. (ed.) *Political Philosophy*. London: Oxford U. Press, 1967. 201 p. [Reprints the Peters and Winch articles from *Proceedings* above.]

RAMM, B. *The Pattern of Authority*. Grand Rapids: Eerdmans, 1957. 117 p.

RAPHAEL, D. D. *Problems of Political Philosophy*. New York: Praeger, 1970. 207 p. [Chap. III, "Sovereignty, Power and Authority"; Chap. V, "Liberty and Authority."]

RAPOPORT, R. N. and R. S. RAPOPORT. " 'Democratization' and Authority in a Therapeutic Community," *Behavioral Science*, II (1957), 128-33.

RAWLINSON, A. E. J. *Authority and Freedom*. London, New York: Longmans, Green and Co., 1924. 189 p.

REIK, T. *Dogma and Compulsion: Psychoanalytic Studies of Religion and Myths*. Trans. by Bernard Miall. New York: International Universities Press, 1951. 332 p.

REIMAN, J. H. *In Defense of Political Philosophy: A Reply to Robert Paul Wolff's "In Defense of Anarchism."* New York: Harper Torchbooks, 1972. 87 p.

REMMERS, H. H. (ed.) *Anti-democratic Attitudes in American Schools.* Evanston, Ill.: Northwestern U. Press, 1963. 344 p. Bibliog.: pp. 324-344.

RENSI, G. *La filosofía dell 'autorità.* Palermo: R. Sandron, 1920. 245 p.

RHODES, C. (ed.) *Authority in a Changing Society.* London: Constable, 1969. 213 p.

RICH, E. C. *Spiritual Authority in the Church of England: An Enquiry.* London, New York: Longmans, Green, 1953. 218 p.

ROBERTS, A. "On Commending Authority," *Blackfriars,* XXXIV (1953), 259-64.

ROBERTS, T. D. *Black Popes: Authority, Its Use and Abuse.* New York: Sheed and Ward, 1954. 139 p.

ROBIN, G. *Le Déclin de l'autorité et la jeunesse actuelle; les causes et les remèdes.* Paris: Wesmael-Charlier, 1962. 136 p.

ROGERS, L. "Authority and Liberty," *Proceedings of the American Philosophical Society,* XCV (1951), 504-11.

ROGHMANN, K. *Dogmatismus und Autoritarismus. Kritik der theoretischen Ansätze und Ergebnisse dreier westdeutscher Untersuchungen.* Meisenhein am Glan: Hain, 1966. 439 p. Bibliog.: pp. 323-330.

ROKEACH, M. *The Open and Closed Mind: Investigations into the Nature of Belief Systems and Personality Systems.* In collaboration with Richard Bonier [and others]. New York: Basic Books, 1960. 447 p. Bibliog.: pp. 421-432.

ROMAN, F. "L'Autorité dans les écoles," *Annales de l'Institut international de sociologie,* XV (1928), 161-65.

RONDET, M. "Le Concile appel à la liberté des Chrétiens," *Pédogogie,* XXI (1966), 607-692.

ROSENSTOCK-HUESSY, E. "Youth and Authority." Chap I in Winslow, T. and F. Davidson, *American Youth,* Cambridge, Mass.: Harvard U. Press, 1940. 216 p.

ROTH, L. "Authority, Religion and Law," *Hibbert Journal,* LVIII (1959-60), 115-20.

ROVER, D. "Freedom and Authority in Our Time," *Thomist,* XVI (1953), 565-82.

RUSSELL, B. R. *Authority and the Individual.* New York: Simon and Schuster, 1949. 79 p.

RUSSELL, B. "Freedom or Authority in Education," *Century,* CIX (1924), 172-80.

RUSSELL, B. "Power, Ancient and Modern," *Political Quarterly,* VIII (1937), 155-164.

SABATIER, A. *The Religions of Authority and the Religion of the Spirit.* Trans. by L. S. Houghton. New York: Hodder & Stoughton, 1904. 410 p.

SABINE, G. H. *History of Political Theory.* 3rd ed. New York: Holt, Rinehart and Winston, 1961. 948 p.

SALVAIRE, J. *Autorité et liberté.* Montpellier: Imprimerie de la charité, 1932. 116 p. Bibliog.: pp. 111-113.

SAMPSON, G. "Authority and the Schools," *Spectator,* CLVII (1937), 703-4.

SANFORD, F. H. *Authoritarianism and Leadership: A Study of the Follower's Orientation to Authority.* Philadelphia: Printed by Stephenson-Brothers, 1950. 189 p. Bibliog.: pp. 187-189.

SANTAYANA, G. "Rational authority" [p. 310-15]; "Rival Seats of Authority" [p. 321-25], in his *Dominations and Powers,* New York: Scribners, 1951.

SANTAYANA, G. "The Revival of Authority" in his *Physical Order and Moral Liberty,* ed. by J. and S. Lachs. Nashville: Vanderbilt U. Press, 1969. [pp. 250-59.]

SANTORO, A. "In tema di ordini legittimi dell'autorità", *Giustizia penale,* LXII (1957), Pt. 2, 879-884.

SANZ y ESCARTIN, E. "De l'Autorité et de la hiérarchie sociale," *Annales de l'Institut international de sociologie,* XV (1928), 135-47.

SCHAAR, J. H. *Escape from Authority: The Perspectives of Erich Fromm.* New York: Basic Books, 1961. 349 p.

SCHAFFNER, B. H. *Father land: A Study of Authoritarianism in the German Family.* New York: Columbia U. Press, 1948. 203 p. Bibliog.: pp. 197-8.

SCHERER, J. B. *Vierhundert Jahre Index Romanus; ein Gang durch den Friedhof Katholischen Geisteslebens nebst einer zeitgemässen Betrachtung über Autorität und Freiheit.* Dusseldorf: Progress-Verlag, 1957. 36 p.

SCHILLER, M. "Political Authority, Self-Defense, and Pre-Emptive War," *Canadian Journal of Philosophy,* I (1972), 409-26.

SCHLITZER, A. L. (ed.) *Apostolic Dimensions of the Religious Life.* Notre Dame: U. of Notre Dame Press, 1966. 168 p.

SCHMIDT-FREYTAG, C. G. *Die Autorität und die Deutschen.* Hrsg. von C. G. Schmidt-Freytag. München: Delp, 1966. 155 p.

SCHNEIDER, H. W. "Santayana and Realistic Conceptions of Authority," *Journal of Philosophy,* XLIX (1952), 214-20.

SCHWARTZ, T. (ed.) *Freedom and Authority: An Introduction to Social and Political Philosophy.* Encino, California: Dickenson Publishing

Co., 1973. 426 p.

SCOTT, W. R. [et al.] "Organizational Evaluation and Authority," *Administrative Science Quarterly,* XII (1967), 93-117.

SERRANO, GUIRADO, E. "Les incompatibilidades de autoridades y funcionarios," *Revista de administración pública,* VII (1956), 59-158.

SHARP, D. L. "Education for Authority," *Atlantic Monthly,* CXXVIII (1921), 13-21.

SHARPE, C. M. *The Normative Use of Scripture by Typical Theologians of Protestant Orthodoxy in Great Britain and America.* Menasha, Wisc.: George Banta Pub. Co., 1912. 77 p.

SHAW, G. C. "The Language of Authority," *Journal of the Royal United Service Institution,* LXXXI (1936), 389-96.

SHERWOOD, J. J. *Authoritarianism and Moral Realism.* Lafayette, Ind.: Herman C. Krannert Graduate School of Industrial Administration, Purdue U., 1965.

SHKLAR, J. N. "Rousseau's Images of Authority," *American Political Science Review,* LVIII (1964), 919-32.

SHUSTER, G. N. (ed.) *Freedom and Authority in the West.* Notre Dame: U. of Notre Dame Press, 1967. 199 p. [Includes articles by J. C. Murray and others.]

SHUTTLEWORTH, P. N. *Not Tradition, but Scripture.* 2d ed. London: J. G. F. & J. Rivington, 1839. 167 p.

SIEGEL, S. "Certain Determinants and Correlates of Authoritarianism," in *Genetic Psychology Monographs,* Provincetown, Mass.: Journal Press, 1954. [Volume 49, p. 187-229.]

SILBERMAN, L. H. "Paradoxes of Freedom and Authority," *Hibbert Journal,* LX (1962), 297-304.

SIMMONS, E. J. "Some Thoughts on the Soviet Concept of Authority and Freedom," *Antioch Review,* XI (1951), 449-60.

SIMON, H. A "Authority," in Conrad Arensberg et al., eds., *Research in Industrial Human Relations,* New York: Harper & Brothers, 1957. 213 p.

SIMON, Y. "Common Good and Common Action," *Review of Politics,* XXII (1960), 202-44.

SIMON, Y. "The Essential Functions of Authority: Excerpt from "The Philosophy of Democratic Government" in Caponigri, A. R. ed. *Modern Catholic Thinkers,* New York: Harper, 1960. [pp. 351-71.]

SIMON, Y. *Freedom and Community.* Ed. by Charles P. O'Donnell. New York: Fordham U. Press, 1968. 201 p.

SIMON, Y. *A General Theory of Authority,* with an introduction by A.

Robert Caponigri. Notre Dame: U. of Notre Dame Press, 1962. 167 p.

SIMON, Y. "Liberty and Authority," *American Catholic Philosophical Association Proceedings*, XV (1940), 86-114.

SIMON, Y. *Nature and Functions of Authority*. Milwaukee: Marquette U. Press, 1940. 78 p.

SIMON, Y. "Thomism and Democracy" in *Conference on Science, Philosophy and Religion*. 2d Symposium. New York, Distributed by Harpers, 1941. [pp. 258-72.]

SLATTERY, C. L. *The Authority of Religious Experience*. New York: Longmans, Green, and Co., 1912. 299 p.

SORLEY, W. R. "Scope of Authority in Science, Morality, and Art," *Modern Churchman*, XIX (1929), 348-57.

SOUTHGATE, W. M. *John Jewel and the Problem of Doctrinal Authority*. Cambridge, Mass.: Harvard U. Press, 1962. 236 p.

SPENCER, M. E. "Weber on Legitimate Norms and Authority," *The British Journal of Sociology*, XXI (1970), 123-34.

SPITZ, D. *Patterns of Anti-democratic Thought: An Analysis and a Criticism, with Special Reference to the American Political Mind in Recent Times*. New York: Macmillan Co., 1949. 304 p.

STAHL, O. G. "More on the Network of Authority," *Public Administration Review*, XX (1960), 35-37.

STANTON, V. H. *The Place of Authority in Matters of Religious Belief*. London and New York: Longmans, Green, 1891. 229 p.

STEIN, L. "The Sociology of Authority," *American Socioligcal Society Proceedings and Publications*, XVIII (1923), 116-20.

STERNBERGER, D. *Autorität, Freiheit und Befehlsgewalt*. Tübingen: J. C. B. Mohr, 1959. 23 p.

STERRETT, J. M. *The Freedom of Authority*. New York and London: Macmillan, 1905. 319 p.

STERRETT, J. M. *Reason and Authority in Religion*. New York: T. Whittaker, 1891. 184 p.

STIRNER, M. *The Ego & His Own: The Case of the Individual Against Authority*. Tr. by S. T. Byington. Revised and introduced by J. Carroll. New York: Harper, 1971. 266 p.

STRACHAN, R. H. *The Authority of Christian Experience: A Study in the Basis of Religious Authority*. London: Student Christian Movement, 1929. 255 p.

STRICKLAND, D. A. "Authority as a Reference Problem," *Ethics*, LXXX (1970), 238-9.

STROHAL, R. *Autorität, ihr Wesen und ihre Funktion im Leben der Gemeinschaft; eine psychologisch-pädagogische Darstellung*. Zürich:

Internationales Institut für Kunstwissenschaften, 1961. 168 p. Bibliog.: pp. 167-168.

STROHAL, R. [et al.] *Autorität—was ist das heute? Umstrittene Machtansprüche in Staat, Gesellschaft und Kultur.* München: Ehrenwirth, 1965. 173 p.

STURZO, L. "Authority and Democracy," *Dublin Review,* CCXX (1942), 151-63.

SULLIVAN, ST. C. *The Concept of Authority in Contemporary Educational Theory.* Washington, D. C.: Catholic U. of America Press, 1952. 239 p. Bibliog.: pp. 207-236.

SUTTER, J. M., H. LUCCIONI. "Le syndrome de la carence d'autorité," *Annales médico-psychologiques.* CXV (1957), 897-901.

TAVARD, G. H. *Holy Writ or Holy Church: The Crisis of the Protestant Reformation.* London: Burns & Oates, 1959. 250 p.

TEN HOOR, M. "Anarchism and Political Authority," *Journal of Social Philosophy,* IV (1939), 177. [A rejoinder to a comment on his paper "Medievalism in Contemporary Political Thought," *ibid.,* III (1938), 342-49.]

TERRIS, M. "On Authority and Education," *Philosophy of Education: Proceedings,* XXVIII (1972), 246-55.

THOMAS, S. B., JR. "Authority and the Law in the United States, 1968," *Ethics,* LXXIX (1969), 115-30.

THOMASON, A. P. "Authority, Order, Discipline, Loyalty," *Antioch Review,* V (1945), 135-42.

THOMPSON, J. D. "Authority and Power in 'Identical' Organizations," *American Journal of Sociology,* LXII (1956), 290-301

THOMPSON, S. M. "Authority of Law," *Ethics,* LXXV (1964), 16-24. [Reply: H. Moulds, LXXVII (1967), 220-3.]

THOULESS, R. H. *Authority and Freedom; Some Pscyhological Problems of Religious Belief.* London: Hodder and Stoughton, 1954. 124 p.

TILLIETTE, X. "La Tentation de l'autorité," in *L'Emeneutica della Libertà Religiosa,* Padova: Cedam, 1968. [pp. 177-195.]

TITUS, H. "Authority and Experimentation", Chap. IX of his *Ethics for Today,* New York: American Book Company, 1936.

TODD, J. M. (ed.) *Problems of Authority:The papers read at an Anglo-French Symposium held at the Abbey of Notre-Dame du Bec, in April, 1961.* Baltimore: Helicon Press, 1962. 260 p. [Includes articles by E. Anscombe and others.]

TORBET, R. "Authority and Obedience in the Church Today," *New Blackfriars,* L (1969), 582-88; 626-32.

TOULEMONDE, J. *Essai sur la psychologie de l'autorité personnelle: Etude d'interpsychologie et de pédagogie.* Paris: Bloud et Gay, 1929. 321 p.

TRENT, W. P. *The Authority of Criticism, and Other Essays.* New York: C. Scribner's Sons, 1899. 291 p.

TRUEBLOOD, D. E. "The Tests of Authority" *Christendom*, II (1937), 424-434.

TRUEBLOOD, D. E. *The Trustworthiness of Religious Experience.* London: G. Allen & Unwin, Ltd., 1939. 93 p.

TUCKER, R. C. "The Theory of Charismatic Leadership," *Daedalus*, XCVII (1968), 731-56.

TUCKER, W. J. *The Function of the Church in Modern Society.* Boston and New York: Houghton Mifflin Co., 1911. 109 p.

ULLMANN, W. *Principles of Government and Politics in the Middle Ages.* London: Methuen, 1961. 320 p.

VALENSIN, A. "Le principe d'autorité et les exigences sociales du temps présent," *Etudes*, LVII (1920), 513-36.

VASSE, D. "L'Autorité du maître, *Etudes*, CCCXXVI (1967), 274-288.

VEDEL, G. "Crises de l'autorité", *Etudes* CCLXXXVIII (1956), 5-21.

VERGHESE, T. P. *The Freedom of Man: An Inquiry into Some Roots of the Tension Between Freedom and Authority in Our Society.* Philadelphia: Westminster Press, 1972. 157 p.

VIOLETT-BUCH *Zur Obrigkeitsschrift von Bischof Dibelius; Dokumente zur Frage der Obrigkeit.* 3. Aufl. Frankfurt am Main: Stimme Verlag, 1963. 124 p.

VOEGELIN, E. *Der autoritäre Staat; ein Versuch über das österreichische Staatsproblem.* Wien: J. Springer, 1936. 289 p. "Literaturverzeichnis": pp. 286-289.

WALSH, W. H. "Knowledge in Its Social Setting," *Mind*, LXXX (1971), 321-36.

WARD, W. "The Philosophy of Authority in Religion" *Hibbert Journal*, I (1902-3), 677-92.

WARFIELD, B. B. "Augustine's Doctrine of Knowledge and Authority," *Princeton Theological Review*, V (1907), 353-397, 529-578.

WASSON, I. "Authority vs. Experience," *Religious Education*, XXXIII (1938), 144-149.

WATT, L. "Rights and Function of Civil Authority," *Month*, 1930, 328-36.

WEBER, M. *Economy and Society: An Outline of Interpretive Sociology.* Ed. and introduced by G. Roth and C. Wettich. Tr. by E. Fischoff [et al]. New York: Bedminster Press, 1968. 3 v.

WEBER, M. *From Max Weber: Essays on Sociology.* Trans., ed. and introduction by H. H. Gerth and C. Wright Mills. New York: Oxford U. Press, 1946. 490 p.

WEBER, M. *Max Weber on Charisma and Institution Building: Selected Papers.* Ed. and with an introd. by S. N. Eisenstadt. Chicago: U. of Chicago Press, 1968. 313 p. Bibliog.: pp. 311-313.

WEBER, M. "The Types of Authority" in *Theories of Society,* ed. T. Parsons, et al. New York: Free Press, 1961. 2v. [I:626-632.]

WEBER, M. *The Theory of Social and Economic Organizations.* Trans. by A. M. Henderson and Talcott Parsons. Glencoe, Ill.: The Free Press, 1957. 436 p.

WELDON, T. D. *The Vocabulary of Politics.* Baltimore: Penguin Books, 1953. 199 p.

WESTBY, D. L. "Typology of Authority in Complex Organizations," *Social Forces,* XLIV (1966), 484-91.

WHITE, J., R. ALTER, and M. RARDIN. "Authoritarianism, Dogmatism, and Usage of Conceptual Categories," *Journal of Personality and Social Psychology,* II (1965), 293-95.

WIEMAN, H. N. "Authority and the Normative Approach," *Journal of Religion,* XVI (1936), 175-202.

WIESER, F. *Das gesetz der macht.* Wien: J. Springer, 1926. 562 p.

WIGGLESWORTH, E. *The Authority of Tradition.* Boston: Thomas & John Fleet, 1778. 39 p.

WIJEYEWARDENE, G. (ed.) *Leadership and Authority: A Symposium.* Singapore: U. of Malaya Press, 1968. 337 p.

WILLIAMS, R. R. *Authority in the Apostolic Age with Two Essays on the Modern Problem of Authority.* London: SCM Press, 1950. 144 p.

WILLOUGHBY, W. W. *The Ethical Basis of Political Authority.* New York: Macmillan, 1930. 460 p.

WILSON, F. G. *The Elements of Modern Politics: An Introduction to Political Science.* New York and London: McGraw-Hill Book Co., Inc., 1936. 716 p.

WILSON, F. G. "The Prelude to Authority," *American Political Science Review,* XXXI (1937), 12-27.

WILSON, J. A. [et al.] *Authority and Law in the Ancient Orient.* Baltimore: American Oriental Society, 1954. 55 p.

WOLFF, R. P. *In Defense of Anarchism.* New York: Harper Torchbooks, 1970. 86. p.

WOLFF, R. P. (ed.) *Political Man and Social Man: Readings in Political Philosophy.* New York: Random House, 1966. 489 p.

WOLPERT, J. F. "Toward a Sociology of Authority" in A. W. Gouldner (ed.) *Studies in Leadership,* New York: Russell & Russell, 1965. [pp. 679-701.]

WOOLF, B. L. *The Authority of Jesus and Its Foundation.* London: Allen and Unwin, Ltd., 1929. 301 p. Bibliog.: pp. 287-290.

WRIGHT, J. "Reflections on Conscience and Authority," *Critic,* XXII (1964), 11-15, 18-28.

WUNBERG, G. *Autorität und Schule.* Stuttgart, Berlin, Köln, Mainz: Kohlhammer, 1966. 87 p.

YÁÑEZ, E. *La autoridad y la libertad en la constitución política del estado; discurso de incorporacion a la Academia chilena correspondiente de la Real Academia española en reemplayo de Don Enrique Mac Iver.* Paris: Editorial "Le Livre libre," 1928. 96 p.

YELAJA, S. A. (ed.) *Authority and Social Work: Concept and Use.* Toronto: U. of Toronto Press, 1971. 309 p.

ZACHARIAS, H. C. E. "Infallibility: Stalinist and Papal," *Blackfriars,* XXXI (1950), 471-4.

ZAHN, G. C. "The Private Conscience and Legitimate Authority," *Commonweal,* LXXVI (1962), 9-13.

ZAHN, G. "The Private Conscience and Legitimate Authority," *New Blackfriars,* XLVIII (1966), 188-200.

[Compilation of this bibliography was completed in 1973.]

Index

171